LUKE DIXON

Luke Dixon is a director, teach
internationally known for both
and site-specific work. He has directed and led workshops on
Shakespeare around the world, from *A Midsummer Night's
Dream* in Brazil to *Macbeth* in Hong Kong via *Pericles* in
South Africa.

Luke is also editor of *Shakespeare Monologues for Men*, *Women*
and *Young Women* in this series, and author of *Play-Acting:
A Guide to Theatre Workshops*. For more information, see
www.lukedixon.co.uk

THE GOOD AUDITION GUIDES

CLASSICAL MONOLOGUES
edited by Marina Caldarone

SHAKESPEARE MONOLOGUES
edited by Luke Dixon

SHAKESPEARE MONOLOGUES FOR YOUNG PEOPLE
edited by Luke Dixon

MODERN MONOLOGUES
edited by Trilby James

The Good Audition Guides

SHAKESPEARE MONOLOGUES FOR YOUNG MEN

edited and introduced by

LUKE DIXON

NICK HERN BOOKS

London

www.nickhernbooks.co.uk

A NICK HERN BOOK

The Good Audition Guides:
Shakespeare Monologues for Young Men
first published in Great Britain in 2012
by Nick Hern Books Limited
The Glasshouse, 49a Goldhawk Road, London W12 8QP

Reprinted 2014, 2015, 2016

Introduction copyright © 2012 Luke Dixon
Copyright in this selection © 2012 Nick Hern Books Ltd

Cover design: www.energydesignstudio.com

Typeset by Nick Hern Books, London
Printed and bound by CPI Group (UK) Ltd

A CIP catalogue record for this book
is available from the British Library

ISBN 978 1 84842 265 0

Contents

6

THE HISTORIES

THE TRAGEDIES

Introduction

The basic requirements for most auditions, from drama-school entry to a season with the Royal Shakespeare Company, will include a speech by Shakespeare. Faced with the thirty-eight plays that are generally considered to have been written by Shakespeare, it is daunting for even the most experienced actor to know where to begin in finding a suitable speech.

The Shakespearean canon, that is all the plays he wrote which have survived, are the heart of English drama. A speech from one of those plays can provide an actor with opportunities to show off their skills and talent in a whole range of ways: vocally and physically, in terms of characterisation and storytelling, emotionally and intellectually. A Shakespeare speech is the best tool for an actor to demonstrate their craft and for an audition panel or director to appreciate and judge it.

SHAKESPEARE AND HIS STAGE ☞

William Shakespeare was born in 1564 in Stratford-upon-Avon and went to the local school. He married Anne Hathaway in 1582. William was eighteen, Anne twenty-six. Their daughter Susanna was born the following year, and twins Hamnet and Judith in 1585. What happened next remains a mystery but eight years later Shakespeare was working successfully in the theatre in London and by the age of thirty was co-owner, actor, and main playwright for London's leading theatre company, the Lord Chamberlain's Men. After James I came to the throne in 1603 they became known as the King's Men. The company built their own theatre on the south bank of the Thames and called it The Globe. A modern replica stands near the site of the original.

It was for that theatre that Shakespeare wrote his best-known plays. They were written to be acted on a stage thrust out into a large crowd standing all around and with banks of seats high up to an open sky. Performing in daylight with little scenery and no lighting, the actors had to create place, time and atmosphere with just their own acting skills and the words given to them by Shakespeare. An actor in the audition room today faces the same challenges, to turn a bare space into an Italian palace (Proteus, *The Two Gentlemen of Verona*), a country pub (Fenton, *The Merry Wives of Windsor*), the Forest of Arden (Orlando, *As You Like It*), a field of battle (*Henry V*), or a castle at dead of night (*Hamlet*).

Thirty-six of Shakespeare's plays were collected after his death by his colleagues and printed in what is known as the First Folio, a folio being the size of the sheet of paper it was printed on. A thousand copies were printed and they sold for £1 each. About 230 still exist and now sell for around £3 million each. A couple of other plays only appeared in what are known as quarto editions, on paper folded to half the size of a folio sheet. For publication, each of the plays was divided into five parts, known as acts. The first act was the introduction or exposition, the second a development of the action, the third a climax or crisis, the fourth more development, and the fifth a resolution. The acts are usually divided into a number of smaller parts called scenes.

THE SPEECHES IN THIS BOOK ☞

This is one of two books of Shakespeare speeches for young people: one for young men and one for young women. There are two companion volumes of speeches for older actors. All the speeches were first spoken by boys and young men – there were no female actors in Shakespeare's day – so it can sometimes be interesting to consider boys' speeches if you are a girl, and girls' speeches if you are a boy. Some characters (citizens, for example, or supernatural creatures) can be thought of as gender neutral – that is, appropriate to be played by either men or women. Some of these characters (though with different speeches) can be found in both this volume and the companion volume of speeches for young women.

The speeches vary greatly in length. There are some very short pieces for those who find the task of learning lines difficult. In some cases there are short speeches which can easily be joined together by the more adventurous young actor to create something more substantial.

CHOOSING YOUR SPEECH ☞

In this volume I have brought together forty speeches, from amongst the best known to the least common. You will never find a 'new' Shakespeare speech. Fashion and contemporary performance are often factors in which speeches are currently popular and you can never second-guess what speech the actor before or after you will perform. Best to find a speech that you like, enjoy performing, and can in some way empathise with. Do not worry about what other actors are doing.

Choose more than one speech to have in your repertoire so that you always have something suitable when the call comes. Having chosen a speech, read the play, and find the backstory so you know where the character and the speech are coming from.

Once you have found a speech that you like and that you think suits you, get hold of a copy of the complete play so that you can work on the speech in context. If that seems daunting, find a film of the play to watch first. There are innumerable editions of the plays of Shakespeare. Those editing them often disagree about the numbering of the scenes and lines. So do not be surprised if the copy of the play that you are using does not agree exactly with the act, scene, and line numbers given in this book.

Complexity   Some of the speeches in this book are relatively simple and might be more useful for the actor for whom Shakespeare is a new and terrifying experience. Lysander in *A Midsummer Night's Dream* and Romeo in *Romeo and Juliet* perhaps fall into this category. Others, such as Mercutio in *Romeo and Juliet* and Laertes in *Hamlet*, are rich and complex

in the language, thought or emotion and might be more
suitable for actors seeking a challenge or needing to show the
full range of their abilities.

Age   It is rare that we know the age of a character in a play
by Shakespeare. In a production the director will have made
decisions about the age of his characters and their relative
ages to each other. In an audition you can be much more
flexible in deciding whether the speech of a character is suited
to you and your playing age.

Length   The speeches vary considerably in the number of
their words but not necessarily in the time they take to
perform. Ferdinand's speech from *The Tempest* is quite short
in the number of words, but contains a good deal of implied
action as he piles his logs. Caliban's speech about the noises
on the island in *The Tempest* is very short but there are sounds
that he needs time to listen to. It is a speech that needs to be
given space to breathe and for the spaces, sounds and silences
within it to be found. In these and many other speeches there
are important moments when the character is listening or
when he is waiting for or expecting a reply (Murellus in *Julius
Caesar*, the Fairy in *A Midsummer Night's Dream*). These
moments between the words can make a speech come fully
alive. Where some speeches are too long for audition purposes
I have, as judiciously as possible, made cuts.

LANGUAGE ☞

Shakespeare's audiences went to 'hear' plays. It was not until
long after his death that anyone wrote of going to 'see' a play.
So the sounds of Shakespeare's words are as important as
their meanings. Indeed the sounds often help convey the
meanings. Enjoy and play with the sounds as you work
through the speeches.

Prose is everyday speech but Shakespeare often heightens that
speech, giving it colour, richness, images and so on that we
would not use in our everyday lives.

Poetry is where that heightened use of language is taken further and the speech goes beyond the everyday and rhythm becomes important.

Verse is poetry where the rhythms of the words are organised.

Iambic pentameter is a particular kind of verse. An 'iamb' is where a short syllable is followed by a long syllable giving a 'di-dum' rhythm. 'Metre' is how rhythms are organised in lines of verse. 'Penta' is the old Greek word for five. So if you put five iambs in a line of verse you get an iambic pentameter:

di-dum, di-dum, di-dum, di-dum, di-dum

This was the main form Shakespeare used in writing his plays: it is the heartbeat of his language. Sometimes it is used rigidly and is easy to spot:

O, then I see Queen Mab has been with you.
She is the fairies' midwife and she comes

(Mercutio, *Romeo and Juliet*)

Sometimes, especially as he got older and more experienced, he played with the form and pulled it around for emotional, dramatic or characterisation effect.

In order for the rhythm to work a word ending in '-*ed*' will sometimes have the letters stressed as a syllable (in which case it is printed '-*èd*'), and sometimes it will not be a separate syllable but be spoken as if the 'e' is not there (in which case it is printed '-'*d*').

Rhyming couplets Sometimes Shakespeare uses rhyme and when two lines together rhyme we have a rhyming couplet. Often these are used at the end of a speech or scene to indicate finality.

Punctuation in Shakespeare is a controversial subject. Shakespeare did not prepare his plays for publication and therefore the punctuation in the texts is largely put there by his colleagues or the publisher or printer. Nonetheless, the punctuation in these speeches, following for the most part the First Folio, can give you some help not just with sense but also with where to breathe, pause, rest, change gear, or change thought.

Vocabulary Shakespeare wrote at a time when English as we know it was developing rapidly. He made up, or used very early in the development of the English language, many words and phrases that have become part of our everyday speech. Words that we find first in Shakespeare include accommodation, critic, dwindle, eventful, exposure, frugal, generous, gloomy, laughable, majestic, misplaced, monumental, multitudinous and obscene. Phrases that he coined include disgraceful conduct, elbow room, fair play, green-eyed monster, clothes make the man, method in his madness, to thine own self be true, the lady doth protest too much, and it's Greek to me. Sometimes he used a word which was never used again. Some of the words he used which are familiar today had different or stronger meanings then than now and these I have glossed in the notes.

THE AUDITION ☞

Thought process It is rare that a character in Shakespeare sets out to make a speech, though in some of the big public and political scenes a character does just that. Lysander in *A Midsummer Night's Dream* has to argue his case in front of the Duke; Murellus in *Julius Caesar* comes out to address the crowds.

But for the most part a speech does start with a single thought which is followed by another and then another until a speech has been said. So allow time for each of those thoughts to come, and be fresh in the mind, before they are spoken. Do not be daunted by what can seem endless lines of text. It is not a race to get through to the end. Take the speech one thought at a time.

Structure As you follow the thoughts, follow too the emotions and language of the speech. Look for its structure. Allow yourself to show the full range of emotion and vocal possibility within the speech. Seek variety. None of these speeches is on one note. All allow a wide range of vocal and emotional expression.

Setting and geography   Many of these speeches are soliloquies allowing the character to express their thoughts or ideas to an audience while he is alone, such as Launcelot Gobbo in *The Merchant of Venice*. Other speeches, like Claudio's in *Measure for Measure*, are parts of dialogues or conversations. And some, such as the First Citizen's in *Coriolanus*, are directed to large public gatherings. Others may be a combination of all these. Decide who else, if anyone, is there to hear the speech and where they are placed in relation to you. Give thought to the geography or layout of the place the speech is being spoken in – be they the woods of *A Midsummer Night's Dream*, Elsinore Castle in *Hamlet*, or the windswept island of *The Tempest*. Take a few moments when you first come into the audition room to place the other characters and recreate the geography and setting in your mind's eye.

Audience   If your speech is directed to an audience, that can be a theatre audience or an audience within the scene. Some speeches are soliloquies which can be played to oneself, to the audience, or some combination of the two (Angelo in *Measure for Measure*). Others are to a public audience within the play (Murellus in *Julius Caesar*). Decide whether and how to use your audition panel as that audience.

Make the space your own   Many other actors will have been in the audition room before you. Many will come after you. Spend a moment or two before you start your speech focusing and allowing the panel to focus on you. Create the silence out of which your words will come and decide on the energy that the words will bring with them, whether Hamlet summoning up the courage to revenge his father's death or the lovelorn Orlando in *As You Like It* finding the places to leave his poems in the forest.

HOW TO USE THIS BOOK

For each speech, as well as specifying who is speaking, I have given an indication of:

WHERE ☞ If possible I have indicated where and when the action is taking place. Sometimes this can be very specific, either because Shakespeare has told us or because the action is tied to a particular historical event. Often the plays are set in times of legend or myth and the date and place are of no direct importance in affecting how you perform them.

WHO ELSE IS THERE ☞ This note gives an indication of who else is on stage and the character's relationship to them.

WHAT IS HAPPENING ☞ This note will give a context for the speech, but it is not a substitute for reading the play and yourself deciding where the speech is coming from.

WHAT TO THINK ABOUT ☞ I have indicated some ideas of things to think about as you are working on the speech. This is by no means an exhaustive list, but will give you a way into the speech and should spark other thoughts and ideas of your own.

WHERE ELSE TO LOOK ☞ If you like a speech or character and want to look elsewhere for similar pieces this note will help you on your way.

GLOSSARY ☞ I have glossed the trickier and perplexing words, phrases and thoughts in the speeches, but do not worry if you need a dictionary or annotated edition of the play to help you fully understand what your character is saying.

THE TEXTS ☞ Wherever possible I have used the exemplary texts of *The Shakespeare Folios* published by Nick Hern Books and edited by Nick de Somogyi (to whom my thanks for his excellent help and advice in editing this volume). Speeches from plays not yet published in this series have been edited by me from the First Folio using the same editorial rules. In the case of *Pericles*, which does not appear in the First Folio, and is of contested authorship, I have used its quarto text edited in the same way. All the glosses are my own.

The following categories may help you find a particular attribute that suits you, or your audition needs:

- HIGH STATUS

    Angelo in *Measure for Measure*
    The Prince of Morocco in *The Merchant of Venice*
    Prince Hal/Henry V in *Henry IV, Parts One and Two*,
        and *Henry V*

- LOW STATUS

    Caliban in *The Tempest*
    Tranio in *The Taming of the Shrew*
    Fabian in *Twelfth Night*
    The Boy in *Henry V*
    The First Citizen in *Coriolanus*

- SONS AND BROTHERS

    Claudio in *Measure for Measure*
    Prince Hal in *Henry IV, Part Two*
    The Son in *Henry VI, Part Three*
    Laertes in *Hamlet*

- IN LOVE

    Ferdinand in *The Tempest*
    Proteus and Valentine in *The Two Gentlemen of Verona*
    Bassanio in *The Merchant of Venice*
    Lorenzo in *The Merchant of Venice*
    Fenton in *The Merry Wives of Windsor*
    Lysander in *A Midsummer Night's Dream*
    Demetrius in *A Midsummer Night's Dream*
    Orlando in *As You Like It*
    Pericles in *Pericles*
    Troilus in *Troilus and Cressida*
    Romeo in *Romeo and Juliet*

- OUT OF LOVE
  Pericles in *Pericles*

- SCARY
  Puck in *A Midsummer Night's Dream*
  Hamlet in *Hamlet*

- COMIC
  Launce in *The Two Gentlemen of Verona*
  Launcelot Gobbo in *The Merchant of Venice*

- ANGRY
  Antonio in *Twelfth Night*
  First Citizen in *Coriolanus*
  Murellus in *Julius Caesar*

- SAD
  The Son in *Henry VI, Part Three*

- SUPERNATURAL
  Ariel in *The Tempest*
  The Fairy in *A Midsummer Night's Dream*
  Puck in *A Midsummer Night's Dream*

The Comedies

The Tempest

WHO ☞ *Ariel, an airy spirit.*

WHERE ☞ *A remote island.*

WHO ELSE IS THERE ☞ *Prospero, the Duke of Milan, who was shipwrecked on the island many years ago.*

WHAT IS HAPPENING ☞ *Ariel is an insubstantial spirit. His master, Prospero, calls him 'thou which art but air'. Yet he has great powers. Prospero was shipwrecked on the island as a result of the treachery of his brother. His brother's ship coming past the island, Prospero has ordered Ariel to create a tempest and wreck it. Here, in the first of two of his speeches in this book, Ariel is reporting back to his master.*

WHAT TO THINK ABOUT ☞

- *How do you portray someone who is an 'airy spirit'?*

- *Ariel takes pleasure in serving Prospero. He has been promised his freedom if he does what he has been asked.*

- *Create a sense of the devastation and fury of the tempest.*

WHERE ELSE TO LOOK ☞ *Another magical creature is Puck (A Midsummer Night's Dream, p. 46).*

Ariel

❝ I boarded the king's ship: now on the beak,*
Now in the waist, the deck, in every cabin,
I flam'd amazement; sometime I'd divide,
And burn in many places; on the topmast,
The yards and bowsprit would I flame distinctly,
Then meet and join. Jove's* lightnings, the precursors
O' th' dreadful thunder-claps, more momentary
And sight-outrunning were not; the fire and cracks
Of sulphurous roaring the most mighty Neptune*
Seem to besiege, and make his bold waves tremble,
Yea, his dread trident* shake.
      Not a soul
But felt a fever of the mad and play'd
Some tricks of desperation. All but mariners
Plung'd in the foaming brine and quit the vessel,
Then all afire with me; the king's son, Ferdinand,
With hair up-staring (then like reeds,* not hair),
Was the first man that leap'd; cried, 'Hell is empty,
And all the devils are here!' **❞**

(Act 1, scene 2, lines 231–52 with cut)

GLOSSARY

beak – bow
Jove – Roman god of thunder and lightning
Neptune – Roman god of the sea
trident – Neptune's three-pronged spear
reeds – burning tapers, spills

The Tempest

WHO ☞ *Ferdinand, son of the King of Naples.*

WHERE ☞ *A remote island.*

WHO ELSE IS THERE ☞ *Ferdinand is alone.*

WHAT IS HAPPENING ☞ *Ferdinand has been shipwrecked and separated from his companions. Prospero, magical master of the island, has imprisoned him and given him hard tasks to do. As he piles up thousands of logs, he thinks of Prospero's daughter Miranda, and the thoughts of her make his work much easier.*

WHAT TO THINK ABOUT ☞

- *Decide if Ferdinand is speaking just to himself or to the audience as well.*

- *Keep an eye open in case Prospero returns.*

- *Feel the weight and size of each log as you move it.*

WHERE ELSE TO LOOK ☞ *Thinking of the girls they love but in very different circumstances, are Bassanio (The Merchant of Venice, p. 56), and Troilus (Troilus and Cressida, p. 90).*

Ferdinand

❝ There be some sports are painful, and their labour
Delight in them sets off:* some kinds of baseness
Are nobly undergone, and most poor matters
Point to rich ends. This my mean task
Would be as heavy to me as odious, but
The mistress which I serve quickens* what's dead,
And makes my labours pleasures. O, she is
Ten times more gentle than her father's crabb'd,*
And he's compos'd of* harshness. I must remove
Some thousands of these logs and pile them up,
Upon a sore injunction:* my sweet mistress
Weeps when she sees me work, and says such baseness
Had never like executor. I forget;
But these sweet thoughts do even refresh my labours,
Most busy least when I do it.* **❞**

(Act 3, scene 1, lines 1–15)

GLOSSARY

sets off – alleviates
quickens – brings life to
crabb'd – angry, cranky
compos'd of – made of
sore injunction – painful command
Most busy least when I do it – i.e. his thoughts are busiest when he is least
busy working

The Tempest

WHO ☞   *Caliban, 'a savage and deformed slave'.*

WHERE ☞   *A remote island.*

WHO ELSE IS THERE ☞   *Stephano and Trinculo, two drunken servants.*

WHAT IS HAPPENING ☞   *Caliban, a native of the island, was years ago enslaved by Prospero, the shipwrecked Duke of Milan. Stephano and Trinculo have themselves just been shipwrecked on the island and Caliban plots with them to overthrow Prospero. Caliban has a number of speeches in the play of which two are in this book and another in the companion volume of Shakespeare Monologues for Men. Both the speeches in this volume are close to one another in the play and could be joined to make one longer speech. Here is the first.*

WHAT TO THINK ABOUT ☞

- *What shape is Caliban; how does he move and breathe and talk?*

- *What makes him 'savage and deformed'?*

- *What emotions does Caliban feel as he thinks of his mother, and of Prospero's beautiful daughter?*

- *How strong is his hate of Prospero?*

WHERE ELSE TO LOOK ☞   *Launcelot Gobbo (The Merchant of Venice, p. 52) is another disgruntled servant who complains about his master.*

Caliban

❝ Why, as I told thee, 'tis a custom with him,
I' th'afternoon to sleep: there thou mayst brain him,*
Having first seiz'd his books, or with a log
Batter his skull, or paunch him* with a stake,
Or cut his wezand* with thy knife. Remember
First to possess his books, for without them
He's but a sot,* as I am, nor hath not
One spirit to command – they all do hate him
As rootedly* as I. Burn but his books.
He has brave utensils* (for so he calls them),
Which when he has a house, he'll deck withal.*
And that most deeply to consider is
The beauty of his daughter; he himself
Calls her a nonpareil.* I never saw a woman
But only Sycorax my dam,* and she;
But she as far surpasseth Sycorax
As great'st does least. **❞**

(Act 3, scene 2, lines 85–101)

GLOSSARY

brain him – hit him on the head
paunch him – stab him in the guts
wezand – throat
sot – fool
rootedly – to the core
brave utensils – impressive pieces of equipment
deck withal – furnish with
nonpareil – one without compare, paragon
dam – mother

The Tempest

WHO ☞ *Caliban, 'a savage and deformed slave'.*

WHERE ☞ *A remote island.*

WHO ELSE IS THERE ☞ *Stephano and Trinculo, two drunken servants.*

WHAT IS HAPPENING ☞ *Caliban, a native of the island, was years ago enslaved by Prospero, the shipwrecked Duke of Milan. Stephano and Trinculo have themselves just been shipwrecked on the island and Caliban plots with them to overthrow Prospero. Caliban has a number of speeches in the play of which two are in this book and one in the companion volume of Shakespeare Monologues for Men. Both speeches are close to one another in the play and could be joined to make one longer speech. Here is the second.*

WHAT TO THINK ABOUT ☞

- *What shape is Caliban; how does he move and breathe and talk?*

- *What makes him 'savage and deformed'?*

- *What are these 'noises' and where are they coming from?*

WHERE ELSE TO LOOK ☞ *Both Ariel (The Tempest, pp. 20 and 28) and Puck (A Midsummer Night's Dream, p. 46) describe other supernatural phenomena.*

Caliban

66 Be not afeard. The isle is full of noises,
Sounds, and sweet airs, that give delight and hurt not.
Sometimes a thousand twangling instruments
Will hum about mine ears; and sometime voices,
That if I then had wak'd after long sleep,
Will make me sleep again; and then, in dreaming,
The clouds methought would open and show riches
Ready to drop upon me, that when I wak'd
I cried to dream again. **99**

(Act 3, scene 2, lines 132–40)

The Tempest

WHO ☞ *Ariel, an airy spirit.*

WHERE ☞ *A remote island.*

WHO ELSE IS THERE ☞ *Prospero, Duke of Milan, who was shipwrecked on the island many years ago.*

WHAT IS HAPPENING ☞ *Ariel is an insubstantial spirit. His master, Prospero, calls him 'thou which art but air'. Yet he has great powers. Prospero was shipwrecked on the island as a result of the treachery of his brother. His brother's ship coming past the island, Prospero has ordered Ariel to create a tempest and wreck it. Caliban, a monster who lives on the island, has conspired with two of the recently shipwrecked servants to overthrow Prospero. Here, in the second of his speeches in this book, Ariel reports back to Prospero as to how he has thwarted their plans.*

WHAT TO THINK ABOUT ☞

- *How does an airy spirit sound, stand and move?*

- *Ariel takes pleasure in serving Prospero. He has been promised his freedom if he does what he has been asked.*

- *Recreate every moment of the scene Ariel is retelling.*

WHERE ELSE TO LOOK ☞ *Another spirit reporting their activities is Puck (A Midsummer Night's Dream, p. 46).*

Ariel

" I told you, sir, they were red-hot with drinking,
So full of valour that they smote the air
For breathing in their faces, beat the ground
For kissing of their feet; yet always bending
Towards their project.* Then I beat my tabor,*
At which, like unback'd colts,* they prick'd their ears,
Advanc'd their eyelids, lifted up their noses
As they smelt music. So I charm'd their ears
That calf-like they my lowing follow'd, through
Tooth'd briers, sharp furzes,* pricking gorse and thorns,
Which enter'd their frail shins. At last I left them
I'th' filthy-mantled* pool beyond your cell,
There dancing up to th' chins, that the foul lake
O'erstunk their feet.* **"**

(Act 4, scene 1, lines 171–83)

GLOSSARY

bending towards their project – moving towards their intent / goal
tabor – drum
unback'd colts – young and untrained horses
furzes - prickly bushes
filthy-mantled – clogged with foul-smelling slime
the foul lake o'erstunk their feet - the stinking lake smelt worse than their
feet

The Two Gentlemen of Verona

WHO ☞   *Launce, a clownish servant.*

WHERE ☞   *A street in Verona, Italy.*

WHO ELSE IS THERE ☞   *Launce is alone.*

WHAT IS HAPPENING ☞   *Upset at having to leave the city with his master, Launce tells the audience that all his family are prone to tears. Even their cat cries. Only Crab his dog remains dry-eyed. With his shoes, staff and hat as puppets, Launce acts out the members of his family. The part would originally have been played by the clown in Shakespeare's company.*

WHAT TO THINK ABOUT ☞

- *If he and his family are prone to weeping, just how truly sad is Launce?*

- *How intelligent do you think Launce to be?*

- *Find personalities for each of the relatives Launce is talking about.*

- *Play with Launce's confusion as he gets muddled with his shoes and hat.*

WHERE ELSE TO LOOK ☞   *Launcelot Gobbo (The Merchant of Venice, p. 52) is another clownish servant who acts out a story.*

Launce

❝ Nay, 'twill be this hour ere I have done weeping; all the kind* of the Launces have this very fault. I have received my proportion, like the prodigious son,* and am going with Sir Proteus to the Imperial's court. I think Crab, my dog, be the sourest-natured dog that lives: my mother weeping, my father wailing, my sister crying, our maid howling, our cat wringing her hands, and all our house in a great perplexity, yet did not this cruel-hearted cur shed one tear. He is a stone, a very pebble stone, and has no more pity in him than a dog: a Jew would have wept to have seen our parting; why, my grandam,* having no eyes, look you, wept herself blind at my parting. Nay, I'll show you the manner of it. This shoe is my father: no, this left shoe is my father: no, no, this left shoe is my mother: nay, that cannot be so neither: yes, it is so, it is so, it hath the worser sole.* This shoe, with the hole in it, is my mother, and this my father; a vengeance on't! There 'tis: now, sit. This staff is my sister, for, look you, she is as white as a lily and as small as a wand: this hat is Nan, our maid: I am the dog: no, the dog is himself, and I am the dog – Oh! the dog is me, and I am myself; ay, so, so. Now come I to my father: 'Father, your blessing.' Now should not the shoe speak a word for weeping: now should I kiss my father; well, he weeps on. Now come I to my mother: O, that she could speak now like a wood* woman! Well, I kiss her; why, there 'tis; here's my mother's breath up and down. Now come I to my sister; mark the moan she makes. Now the dog all this while sheds not a tear nor speaks a word; but see how I lay the dust with my tears. **❞**

(Act 2, scene 3, from line 1)

GLOSSARY

kind – family
the prodigious son – Launce means the Prodigal Son in the biblical parable
grandam – grandmother
the worser sole – a pun on the state of his mother's soul
wood – furious, mad (perhaps punning on the wooden sole of the shoe he is holding)

The Two Gentlemen of Verona

WHO ☞ *Valentine.*

WHERE ☞ *Milan, a room in the Duke's Palace.*

WHO ELSE IS THERE ☞ *His best friend Proteus.*

WHAT IS HAPPENING ☞ *Valentine is telling Proteus of his love for Silvia and of their plans to elope together.*

WHAT TO THINK ABOUT ☞

- *What is it about Silvia that Valentine loves? Have a picture of her in your mind.*

- *How strong is his friendship with Proteus, and how strong the conflict between his friendship and his love?*

- *Work out the detail of the elopement plan. Is it exciting or dangerous, and if so in what ways?*

WHERE ELSE TO LOOK ☞ *Also declaring their love in different ways are Proteus (The Two Gentlemen of Verona, p. 34), Lysander (A Midsummer Night's Dream p. 42) and Orlando (As You Like It, p. 62).*

Valentine

❝ Pardon me, Proteus.
Why, man, she is mine own,
And I as rich in having such a jewel
As twenty seas, if all their sand were pearl,
The water nectar, and the rocks pure gold.
Forgive me that I do not dream on thee,*
Because thou see'st me dote upon my love.
My foolish rival, that her father likes
Only for* his possessions are so huge,
Is gone with her along, and I must after,
For love, thou know'st, is full of jealousy.
Ay, and we are betroth'd;* nay, more, our marriage-hour,
With all the cunning manner of our flight,
Determin'd of:* how I must climb her window,
The ladder made of cords,* and all the means
Plotted and 'greed on* for my happiness.
Good Proteus, go with me to my chamber,
In these affairs to aid me with thy counsel.* ❞

(*Act 2, scene 4, lines 166–86, with cuts*)

GLOSSARY

dream on thee – i.e. give you my undivided attention
for – because
betroth'd – engaged to be married
Determin'd of – decided upon
ladder made of cords – rope-ladder
'greed on – agreed upon
counsel – advice

The Two Gentlemen of Verona

WHO ☞ *Proteus, a gentleman of Verona.*

WHERE ☞ *The Duke's Palace in Milan.*

WHO ELSE IS THERE ☞ *Proteus is alone.*

WHAT IS HAPPENING ☞ *Proteus has a girlfriend, Julia, and a best friend, Valentine. He has just fallen in love with Silvia, Valentine's girlfriend. Proteus cannot decide what to do for the best. If he loves Silvia he will be breaking his trust with both Julia and Valentine. He tells himself that Julia is just a twinkling star compared to the brightness of Silvia's sun, and that promises made without thought can, with a little careful thought, be broken. In the end his desire outweighs his conscience. Valentine is planning to visit Silvia that night. Proteus decides to warn Silvia's father and say that she and Valentine are planning to run off together.*

WHAT TO THINK ABOUT ☞

- *What do Julia and Sylvia look like, and what is it about one that he prefers over the other?*

- *How strong has his friendship with Valentine been till now? How long have they known each other?*

- *Proteus wrestles with his conscience, but how strong is that conscience compared with his desire?*

WHERE ELSE TO LOOK ☞ *Angelo (Measure for Measure, p. 40) is also caught between conscience and desire.*

Proteus

❝ To leave my Julia, shall I be forsworn;*
To love fair Silvia, shall I be forsworn;
To wrong my friend, I shall be much forsworn;
And even that power which gave me first my oath
Provokes me to this threefold perjury:
Love bade me swear, and Love bids me forswear.
O sweet-suggesting Love, if thou hast sinn'd,

Teach me, thy tempted subject, to excuse it!
At first I did adore a twinkling star,
But now I worship a celestial* sun.
Unheedful vows may heedfully be broken,
And he wants wit that wants resolvèd will
To learn his wit t'exchange the bad for better.
I cannot leave to love,* and yet I do;
But there I leave to love where I should love.
Julia I lose and Valentine I lose:
If I keep them, I needs must lose myself;
If I lose them, thus find I by their loss
For Valentine myself, for Julia Silvia.
I to myself am dearer than a friend,
For love is still most precious in itself;
And Silvia – witness Heaven that made her fair! –
Shows Julia but a swarthy Ethiope.*
I will forget that Julia is alive,
Remembering that my love to her is dead;
And Valentine I'll hold an enemy,
Aiming at Silvia as a sweeter friend.
I cannot now prove constant to myself
Without some treachery us'd to Valentine.
This night he meaneth with a corded ladder*
To climb celestial Silvia's chamber-window,
Myself in counsel, his competitor.*
Now presently I'll give her father notice
Of their disguising and pretended* flight;
Who, all enrag'd, will banish Valentine;
For Thurio, he intends, shall wed his daughter;
Love, lend me wings to make my purpose swift,
As thou hast lent me wit to plot this drift! 🙶

(Act 2, scene 6, lines 1–43, with cuts)

GLOSSARY

be forsworn – break my promise
celestial – heavenly
leave to love – stop myself loving
swarthy Ethiope – dark-skinned African
corded ladder – rope-ladder
Myself in counsel, his competitor – assisting him myself, albeit his rival
pretended – intended

The Merry Wives of Windsor

WHO ☞ *Fenton, a young gentleman.*

WHERE ☞ *The Garter Inn, in the provincial town of Windsor.*

WHO ELSE IS THERE ☞ *The Host of the Inn.*

WHAT IS HAPPENING ☞ *Fenton is in love with Anne Page, daughter of Mistress Page. But her father wants her to marry Slender, the Judge's cousin, and her mother wants her to marry Doctor Caius, a French physician. Anne (or 'Nan') has promised both her parents that she will this night marry the man of their choice. In fact she intends to marry neither but instead run off with Fenton. Fenton tells all this to the landlord of the pub, and asks him to arrange with the vicar to meet them at the church between midnight and one.*

WHAT TO THINK ABOUT ☞

- *This is a long and complicated plot. Make sure you have each of the characters involved clearly in mind, and take care that the Host understands what is planned.*

- *Have a clear picture in your mind of Anne, and what it is that Fenton loves about her.*

- *Fenton is excited. This will affect the way in which he tells everything to the Host. He will also want all this kept secret.*

WHERE ELSE TO LOOK ☞ *Other plotting lovers are Proteus (The Two Gentlemen of Verona, p. 34), Orlando (As You Like It, p. 62) and Troilus (Troilus and Cressida, p 90).*

Fenton

❝ From time to time I have acquainted you
With the dear love I bear to fair Anne Page;
Who mutually hath answer'd my affection,
So far forth as herself might be her chooser,
Even to my wish.*

           Hark, good mine host.

Tonight at Herne's Oak,* just 'twixt twelve and one,
Must my sweet Nan present* the Fairy Queen –
The purpose why is here – in which disguise,
While other jests are something rank on foot,*
Her father hath commanded her to slip
Away with Slender, and with him at Eton
Immediately to marry; she hath consented. Now, sir,
Her mother, ever strong against that match
And firm for Doctor Caius, hath appointed
That he shall likewise shuffle her away,
While other sports are tasking of their minds,
And at the deanery, where a priest attends,
Straight marry her. To this her mother's plot
She, seemingly obedient, likewise hath
Made promise to the doctor. Now, thus it rests:
Her father means she shall be all in white,
And in that habit, when Slender sees his time
To take her by the hand and bid her go,
She shall go with him; her mother hath intended
That quaint* in green she shall be loose enrob'd,
With ribands pendent flaring 'bout her head;*
And when the doctor spies his vantage ripe,
To pinch her by the hand – and, on that token,
The maid hath given consent to go with him.
[She means,] good host, to go along with me:
And here it rests, that you'll procure the vicar
To stay for me at church 'twixt twelve and one,
And, in the lawful name of marrying,
To give our hearts united ceremony. 🙶

(*Act 4, scene 6, lines 8–52, with cuts*)

GLOSSARY

Who mutually… even to my wish – who, insofar as she has any choice in
     the matter at all, reciprocates my love
Herne's Oak – a great oak tree in Windsor Park
present – perform, pretend to be
other jests are something rank on foot – other tricks are proliferating
quaint – elegant, stylish
ribands pendent flaring 'bout her head – decorative ribbons radiating about
     her head

Measure for Measure

WHO ☞ *Claudio, a young gentleman.*

WHERE ☞ *A street in Vienna.*

WHO ELSE IS THERE ☞ *Lucio and a Provost.*

WHAT IS HAPPENING ☞ *Claudio has been arrested by a Provost, an official of the court. His friend Lucio asks him why. Claudio tells him that his offence is to have slept with his girlfriend Julietta before their wedding night. They were contracted to be married but were waiting for a dowry dependent on her friends' approval. Julietta is now pregnant and their affair has been made known. The tyrannical deputy, standing in for the absent Duke of Vienna, is using long-neglected laws to prosecute him.*

WHAT TO THINK ABOUT ☞

- *Does Claudio feel any guilt or shame, or does he just feel badly treated?*

- *What are his feelings about the justice of what the deputy Duke is doing?*

- *Have a picture of Julietta in your mind and what it is about her that has made you risk your life to sleep with her.*

- *What does Claudio think about the pregnancy?*

WHERE ELSE TO LOOK ☞ *Romeo (Romeo and Juliet, p. 96) has a secret love, and Ferdinand (The Tempest, p. 22) is suffering punishment for his love.*

Claudio

❝ Thus stands it with me: upon a true contract
I got possession of Julietta's bed:
You know the lady; she is fast* my wife,
Save that we do the denunciation lack
Of outward order.* This we came not to
Only for propagation of a dower*
Remaining in the coffer* of her friends,
From whom we thought it meet to hide our love
Till time had made them for us. But it chances
The stealth of our most mutual entertainment
With character too gross is writ on Juliet.*
And the new Deputy now for the Duke –
Whether it be the fault and glimpse of newness,
Or whether that the body public be
A horse whereon the governor doth ride,
Who, newly in the seat, that it may know
He can command, lets it straight feel the spur;
Whether the tyranny be in his place,
Or in his eminence that fills it up,
I stagger in – but this new governor
Awakes me all the enrollèd penalties
Which have, like unscour'd armour, hung by the wall
So long that nineteen zodiacs* have gone round,
And none of them been worn; and, for a name
Now puts the drowsy and neglected act
Freshly on me. 'Tis surely for a name.* **❞**

(Act 1, scene 2, lines 133–59, with cuts)

GLOSSARY

fast – almost
Save… outward order – we just lack the public formalities
propagation of a dower – increase in the marriage settlement
coffer – chest
it chances… writ on Juliet – it turns out that Juliet became pregnant,
    which is now obvious, as a result of our secret tryst
zodiacs – star signs, i.e. years
for a name – to earn a reputation

Measure for Measure

WHO ☞ *Angelo, Lord Deputy to the Duke of Vienna.*

WHERE ☞ *A room in Angelo's house.*

WHO ELSE IS THERE ☞ *Angelo is alone.*

WHAT IS HAPPENING ☞ *The Duke of Vienna has left the city and Angelo is deputising in his absence. The power has gone to his head. Obsessed with Isabel, a young girl about to become a nun, he can think of nothing else. Isabel's brother Claudio has slept with his girlfriend before they are married, an offence for which Angelo can have him executed. Angelo has offered to spare Claudio if Isabel will sleep with him.*

WHAT TO THINK ABOUT ☞

- *What is it about Isabel that Angelo is obsessed with?*

- *How much is he struggling with his conscience and how strong is his desire?*

- *Are these feelings of sexual desire new to Angelo, or is it his new power that releases them?*

WHERE ELSE TO LOOK ☞ *Struggling with his conscience in a comic way is Launcelot Gobbo (The Merchant of Venice, p. 52). Proteus (The Two Gentlemen of Verona, p. 34) also has a moral dilemma.*

Angelo

❝ When I would pray and think, I think and pray
To several subjects. Heaven hath my empty words
Whilst my invention,* hearing not my tongue,
Anchors on Isabel: Heaven in my mouth,
As if I did but only chew his name;*
And in my heart the strong and swelling evil
Of my conception.* The state whereon I studied
Is like a good thing being often read,
Grown fear'd and tedious. Yea, my gravity,*
Wherein – let no man hear me – I take pride,
Could I with boot change for an idle plume
Which the air beats for vain.* O place, O form,
How often dost thou with thy case, thy habit,*
Wrench awe from fools, and tie the wiser souls
To thy false seeming! Blood, thou art blood.
Let's write 'Good Angel' on the Devil's horn:
'Tis not the Devil's crest.* **❞**

(Act 2, scene 4, lines 1–17)

GLOSSARY

invention – imagination
Heaven in my mouth… chew his name – while simply paying lip-service to
　piety
conception – creative invention
Yea, my gravity… Could I with boot change … beats for vain – i.e. I could
　even usefully exchange the formal dignity of my rank for the change-
　ably frivolous fashions of a foolish lover
case… habit – garment… clothing
Let's write… Devil's crest – i.e. whatever virtuous label we may give to
　our outward appearance, our inner impulse remains the same

A Midsummer Night's Dream

WHO ☞ *Lysander, a young lord in love with Hermia.*

WHERE ☞ *The palace of Theseus, Duke of Athens.*

WHO ELSE IS THERE ☞ *The Duke and his betrothed, Hippolyta; Hermia and her father; and Demetrius, who also loves Hermia.*

WHAT IS HAPPENING ☞ *Lysander and Demetrius are both in love with Hermia. Hermia loves Lysander, but her father wants her to marry Demetrius. They have all come to the palace to ask the Duke to settle the dispute.*

WHAT TO THINK ABOUT ☞

- *Place the other people in the scene and be clear who is being addressed at every point in the speech.*

- *Lysander is sarcastic, clever and full of himself. How much is he showing off in front of everybody?*

- *He stands up for himself in front of the Duke. How difficult is this for him?*

WHERE ELSE TO LOOK ☞ *Romeo (Romeo and Juliet, p. 96) and Orlando (As You Like It, p. 62) are both sure of their love and emboldened by it.*

Lysander

❝ You have her father's love, Demetrius;
Let me have Hermia's: do you marry him.
I am, my lord, as well deriv'd* as he,
As well possess'd;* my love is more than his;
My fortunes every way as fairly rank'd,*
If not with vantage,* as Demetrius';
And, which is more than all these boasts can be,
I am belov'd of beauteous Hermia:
Why should not I then prosecute my right?
Demetrius, I'll avouch it to his head,
Made love to* Nedar's daughter, Helena,
And won her soul; and she, sweet lady, dotes,
Devoutly dotes, dotes in idolatry,
Upon this spotted* and inconstant man. **❞**

(*Act 1, scene 1, lines 93–110, with cut*)

GLOSSARY

as well deriv'd – from as good a family
As well possess'd – as wealthy
as fairly rank'd – of equal status
with vantage – better than
Made love to – courted, wooed
spotted – impure, morally tainted

A Midsummer Night's Dream

WHO ☞ *A Fairy.*

WHERE ☞ *A wood near Athens.*

WHO ELSE IS THERE ☞ *Puck (or Robin Goodfellow), a lowly supernatural spirit.*

WHAT IS HAPPENING ☞ *This is the start of the first scene in the play where we meet the fairy creatures who live in the wood. Puck has come in from one side and met a Fairy coming in the other and asked the Fairy where he is wandering. In the next speech in this book, Puck will tell the fairies about himself.*

WHAT TO THINK ABOUT ☞

- *The pairs of rhyming lines are called 'rhyming couplets'. Think of the speech as a kind of spoken song.*

- *Find a way of moving and speaking that is magical.*

- *The Fairy is enjoying showing off his status as a servant of Titania, the Queen of the Fairies.*

WHERE ELSE TO LOOK ☞ *Other supernatural creatures include Puck (A Midsummer Night's Dream, p. 46) and Ariel (The Tempest, pp. 20 and 28).*

A Fairy

❝ Over hill, over dale,
Thorough bush, thorough brier,
Over park, over pale,*
Thorough flood, thorough fire,
I do wander everywhere,
Swifter than the moon's sphere;
And I serve the Fairy Queen,
To dew her orbs* upon the green.
The cowslips tall her pensioners* be:
In their gold coats spots you see;
Those be rubies, fairy favours,
In those freckles live their savours.*
I must go seek some dewdrops here
And hang a pearl in every cowslip's ear.
Farewell, thou lob* of spirits; I'll be gone:
Our Queen and all our elves come here anon. **❞**

(Act 2, scene 1, lines 2–17)

GLOSSARY

pale – enclosed land
orbs – fairy rings
pensioners – bodyguards
savours – perfumes
lob – rustic buffoon

A Midsummer Night's Dream

WHO ☞ *Puck (or Robin Goodfellow), a mischievous spirit.*

WHERE ☞ *A wood near Athens.*

WHO ELSE IS THERE ☞ *A Fairy.*

WHAT IS HAPPENING ☞ *A Fairy (see previous speech in this book) has just identified Puck as 'that shrewd and knavish sprite, Robin Goodfellow'. Here, Puck tells of the pranks that he plays. Two other Puck speeches can be found in the companion book of Monologues for Girls.*

WHAT TO THINK ABOUT ☞

- *Find ways in which a 'knavish sprite' might sound and move.*

- *Create the character of the old woman that Puck describes playing a trick on.*

- *Puck enjoys showing off to his audience, but then suddenly his mood changes when Oberon enters, and he charges the Fairy to stand aside.*

WHERE ELSE TO LOOK ☞ *Other supernatural creatures are The Fairy in this play (A Midsummer Night's Dream, p. 44) and Ariel (The Tempest, pp. 20 and 28). Both Launce (The Two Gentlemen of Verona, p. 30) and Launcelot Gobbo (The Merchant of Venice, p. 52) dramatise the anecdotes they tell.*

Puck

" [Fairy,] thou speak'st aright;
I am that merry wanderer of the night.
I jest to Oberon and make him smile
When I a fat and bean-fed horse beguile,*
Neighing in likeness of a filly foal;
And sometime lurk I in a gossip's bowl*
In very likeness of a roasted crab,*
And when she drinks, against her lips I bob
And on her wither'd dewlap* pour the ale.
The wisest aunt,* telling the saddest tale,
Sometime for three-foot stool mistaketh me;
Then slip I from her bum, down topples she,
And 'Tailor' cries,* and falls into a cough;
And then the whole choir* hold their hips and laugh,
And waxen* in their mirth and neeze* and swear
A merrier hour was never wasted there.
But room, fairy! Here comes Oberon.* **"**

(Act 2, scene 1, lines 42–58)

GLOSSARY

bean-fed... beguile – well-fed... trick
gossip's bowl – old woman's cup
crab – crab apple
dewlap – double-chin
aunt – old woman
And 'Tailor' cries – a proverbial expression of surprise after a fall (as we
     might say 'Bless you' after a sneeze)
whole choir – entire company
waxen – increase
neeze – sneeze
Oberon – King of the Fairies

A Midsummer Night's Dream

WHO ☞ *Demetrius, a young lord.*

WHERE ☞ *The woods outside Athens.*

WHO ELSE IS THERE ☞ *Duke Theseus, Lysander, Hermia, Helena, and others.*

WHAT IS HAPPENING ☞ *After a night of romantic confusion while lost in the woods, four lovers have just woken up. Lysander and Hermia find themselves in love with one another, as do Demetrius and Helena. Demetrius is telling the Duke what has happened.*

WHAT TO THINK ABOUT ☞

- *How does it feel to wake up and remember things that have happened as if in a dream?*

- *The Duke has the highest status of anyone in Athens. How will this affect the way Demetrius talks to him?*

- *Picture Helena who is suddenly and unexpectedly so attractive. Where is she?*

WHERE ELSE TO LOOK ☞ *Tranio (The Taming of the Shrew, p. 68) declares his love.*

Demetrius

66 My lord, fair Helen told me of their stealth,
Of this their purpose hither to this wood;
And I in fury hither follow'd them,
Fair Helena in fancy following me.
But, my good lord, I wot* not by what power,
But by some power it is, my love to Hermia,
Melted as the snow, seems to me now
As the remembrance of an idle gaud*
Which in my childhood I did dote upon;
And all the faith, the virtue of my heart,
The object and the pleasure of mine eye,
Is only Helena. To her, my lord,
Was I betroth'd ere I saw Hermia:
But like in sickness did I loathe this food;
But, as in health come to my natural taste,
Now I do wish it, love it, long for it,
And will for evermore be true to it. 99

(Act 4, scene 1, lines 163–79)

GLOSSARY

wot – know
idle gaud – silly toy

The Merchant of Venice

WHO ☞ *The Prince of Morocco.*

WHERE ☞ *Portia's house in Belmont, outside Venice.*

WHO ELSE IS THERE ☞ *Portia, her maid Nerissa, and others.*

WHAT IS HAPPENING ☞ *The Prince has come to Belmont to win the young heiress Portia for his wife. Portia explains that her father has laid down a strict condition in his will. He has left three caskets, one of gold, one of silver and one of lead. Only one has Portia's portrait in it. The Prince must choose the correct casket if he is to marry Portia. If he chooses the wrong casket, he can never marry anyone else.*

WHAT TO THINK ABOUT ☞

- *The Prince is a proud soldier. How will this affect his bearing and his manner?*

- *How much does the Prince love Portia, and how much is he attracted by her fortune?*

- *He has an audience that includes Portia, Nerissa and others. Decide how everyone is positioned and who he wants to impress.*

WHERE ELSE TO LOOK ☞ *Bassanio has the same choice to make (The Merchant of Venice, pp. 54 and 56) and Pericles (Pericles, pp. 70 and 72) also has a problem to solve to win a bride.*

The Prince of Morocco

" Mislike me not for my complexion,
The shadow'd livery* of the burnish'd sun,
To whom I am a neighbour and near bred.
Bring me the fairest creature northward born,
Where Phoebus' fire* scarce thaws the icicles,
And let us make incision for your love,
To prove whose blood is reddest, his or mine.
I tell thee, lady, this aspect of mine
Hath fear'd the valiant; by my love I swear,
The best-regarded virgins of our clime
Have lov'd it too. I would not change this hue
Except to steal your thoughts, my gentle queen.
Therefore, I pray you, lead me to the caskets
To try my fortune. By this scimitar*
That slew the Sophy and a Persian prince
That won three fields of Sultan Solyman,
I would outstare the sternest eyes that look,
Outbrave the heart most daring on the earth,
Pluck the young sucking cubs from the she-bear,
Yea, mock the lion when he roars for prey,
To win thee, lady.
　　　　　Good fortune then!
To make me blest or cursed'st among men. **"**

(Act 2, scene 1, lines 1–46, with cuts)

GLOSSARY

livery – badge, token
Phoebus' fire – the rays of the sun (pronounced Fee-bus)
scimitar – curved sword
Sophy – Shah (King) of Persia

The Merchant of Venice

WHO ☞ *Launcelot Gobbo, a comic servant.*

WHERE ☞ *A street in Venice.*

WHO ELSE IS THERE ☞ *Launcelot Gobbo is alone.*

WHAT IS HAPPENING ☞ *Launcelot Gobbo is servant to Shylock, a money lender. Shylock treats him badly and Gobbo is trying to decide whether to run away from his master. The part would originally have been played by the clown or comic in Shakespeare's company.*

WHAT TO THINK ABOUT ☞

- *You could perform this like a modern stand-up comedian.*

- *There are two opposing voices that Gobbo is listening to – a fiend telling him to leave, and his conscience telling him to stay. Find sounds for those voices.*

- *Decide why Gobbo feels the need to escape.*

WHERE ELSE TO LOOK ☞ *Launce (The Two Gentlemen of Verona, p. 30) is another clownish character talking to the audience.*

Launcelot Gobbo

❝ Certainly my conscience will serve me to run from this Jew my master. The fiend* is at mine elbow and tempts me, saying to me, 'Gobbo, Launcelot Gobbo, good Launcelot,' or 'Good Gobbo,' or 'Good Launcelot Gobbo, use your legs, take the start, run away.' My conscience says, 'No, take heed, honest Launcelot; take heed, honest Gobbo,' or, as aforesaid, 'honest Launcelot Gobbo; do not run; scorn running with thy heels.' Well, the most courageous fiend bids me pack: 'Via!'* says the fiend; 'Away!' says the fiend; 'for the heavens, rouse up a brave mind,' says the fiend, 'and run.' Well, my conscience, hanging about the neck of my heart, says very wisely to me, 'My honest friend Launcelot, being an honest man's son –' or rather an honest woman's son; for, indeed, my father did something smack, something grow to, he had a kind of taste; well, my conscience says, 'Launcelot, budge not.' 'Budge,' says the fiend. 'Budge not,' says my conscience. 'Conscience,' say I, 'you counsel well.' 'Fiend,' say I, 'you counsel well': to be ruled by my conscience, I should stay with the Jew my master, who, God bless the mark, is a kind of devil; and, to run away from the Jew, I should be ruled by the fiend, who, saving your reverence, is the devil himself. Certainly the Jew is the very devil incarnal;* and, in my conscience, my conscience is but a kind of hard conscience, to offer to counsel me to stay with the Jew. The fiend gives the more friendly counsel: I will run, fiend; my heels are at your commandment; I will run. **❞**

(Act 2, scene 2, from line 1)

GLOSSARY

fiend – devil
Via! – on your way!
incarnal – in human form

The Merchant of Venice

WHO ☞   *Bassanio, in love with Portia.*

WHERE ☞   *Portia's house in Belmont, outside of Venice.*

WHO ELSE IS THERE ☞   *Portia, her maid Nerissa, Bassanio's friend Gratiano, and others.*

WHAT IS HAPPENING ☞   *Bassanio has come to Belmont to win the young heiress Portia for his wife. Portia explains that her father has laid down a strict condition in his will. He has left three caskets, one of gold, one of silver and one of lead. Only one has Portia's portrait in it. Bassanio must choose the correct casket if he is to marry Portia. If he chooses the wrong casket, he can never marry anyone else.*

WHAT TO THINK ABOUT ☞

- *How much of what Bassanio says is to himself, how much to Portia, and how much to a wider audience?*

- *Where are the caskets and how does he move between them?*

- *How quickly does he make his final choice?*

WHERE ELSE TO LOOK ☞   *The Prince of Morocco has the same choice to make (The Merchant of Venice, p. 50) and Pericles (Pericles, pp. 70 and 72) also has a problem to solve to win a bride.*

Bassanio

❝ So may the outward shows be least themselves:
The world is still* deceiv'd with ornament.
In law, what plea so tainted and corrupt,
But, being season'd with a gracious voice,
Obscures the show of evil? In religion,
What damnèd error, but some sober brow
Will bless it and approve it with a text,
Hiding the grossness with fair ornament?
There is no vice so simple but assumes
Some mark of virtue on his outward parts:

How many cowards, whose hearts are all as false
As stairs of sand, wear yet upon their chins
The beards of Hercules* and frowning Mars,*
Who, inward search'd, have livers white as milk;*
And these assume but valour's excrement*
To render them redoubted!* Look on beauty,
And you shall see 'tis purchas'd by the weight,
Which therein works a miracle in nature,
Making them lightest that wear most of it:
So are those crispèd snaky golden locks
Which make such wanton gambols with the wind
Upon supposèd fairness, often known
To be the dowry of a second head,*
The skull that bred them in the sepulchre.
Thus ornament is but the guilèd* shore
To a most dangerous sea; the beauteous scarf
Veiling an Indian beauty: in a word,
The seeming truth which cunning times put on
To entrap the wisest. Therefore, thou gaudy gold,
Hard food for Midas,* I will none of thee;
Nor none of thee, thou pale and common drudge*
'Tween man and man: but thou, thou meagre lead,
Which rather threaten'st than dost promise aught,
Thy paleness moves me more than eloquence;
And here choose I: joy be the consequence! **99**

(Act 3, scene 2, lines 73–107)

GLOSSARY

still – always
Hercules – the great warrior superhero of classical mythology
Mars – the Roman god of war
livers white as milk – extremely timorous dispositions
valour's excrement – the outward show of bravery
render them redoubted – make them seem strong
the dowry of a second head – i.e. a wig made from another's hair
guilèd – deceptive
Midas – the greedy king of legend who was granted his wish to turn
    everything he touched into gold – but found he could no longer eat
    as a result
drudge – lowly go-between (because silver is used for coins)

The Merchant of Venice

WHO ☞ *Bassanio, in love with Portia.*

WHERE ☞ *Portia's house in Belmont, outside of Venice.*

WHO ELSE IS THERE ☞ *Portia, her maid Nerissa, Bassanio's friend Gratiano, Salerio (a messenger from Venice), and others.*

WHAT IS HAPPENING ☞ *Bassanio has come to Belmont to win the young heiress Portia for his wife. Portia explains that her father has laid down a strict condition in his will. He has left three caskets, one of gold, one of silver and one of lead. Only one has Portia's portrait in it. Bassanio must choose the correct casket if he is to marry Portia. If he chooses the wrong casket, he can never marry anyone else. There are two speeches by Bassanio in this book. In this second one, he has just chosen the correct casket and won both Portia's hand and her heart. But in order to make his journey to Belmont, Bassanio has had to borrow money from his friend Antonio. Antonio in turn has had to borrow money from Shylock, a money lender. Antonio has borrowed the money on the expectation of his wealth arriving by ship to Venice. Bassanio has just read in a letter that Antonio's ships have been lost and that he must surrender a pound of his flesh to settle the debt.*

WHAT TO THINK ABOUT ☞

- *How difficult is it for Bassanio to tell Portia what he has just found out?*

- *Why does he address Portia as 'lady' three times in the speech?*

- *What are Bassanio's feelings for his friend, his lover, and himself?*

WHERE ELSE TO LOOK ☞ *Also having problems in love are Romeo (Romeo and Juliet, p. 96) and Ferdinand (The Tempest, p. 22).*

Bassanio

" O sweet Portia,
Here are a few of the unpleasant'st words
That ever blotted paper! Gentle lady,
When I did first impart my love to you,
I freely told you all the wealth I had
Ran in my veins, I was a gentleman;
And then I told you true. And yet, dear lady,
Rating myself at nothing, you shall see
How much I was a braggart.* When I told you
My state was nothing, I should then have told you
That I was worse than nothing; for indeed
I have engag'd myself to a dear friend,
Engag'd my friend to his mere* enemy,
To feed my means. Here is a letter, lady;
The paper as the body of my friend,
And every word in it a gaping wound
Issuing life-blood. But is it true, Salerio?
Have all his ventures fail'd? What, not one hit?
From Tripolis,* from Mexico and England,
From Lisbon, Barbary,* and India?
And not one vessel 'scape the dreadful touch
Of merchant-marring rocks?* **"**

(Act 3, scene 2, lines 251–71)

GLOSSARY

braggart – boaster
mere – complete, utter
Tripolis – Tripoli, now capital of Libya
Barbary – north Africa
merchant-marring rocks – rocks that sink merchant ships

The Merchant of Venice

WHO ☞ *Lorenzo, in love with Jessica.*

WHERE ☞ *The garden of Portia's house in Belmont, outside Venice.*

WHO ELSE IS THERE ☞ *Jessica, his lover.*

WHAT IS HAPPENING ☞ *Jessica has just run away from her father, Shylock, to elope with Lorenzo. Lorenzo is a Christian, Jessica is a Jew. The two are alone in a beautiful, moonlit garden.*

WHAT TO THINK ABOUT ☞

- *Find a way of being comfortable, intimate, and romantic.*

- *Imagine and place the moon in the sky above you.*

- *What is it that Bassanio loves about Jessica and how difficult has it been for them to escape together?*

WHERE ELSE TO LOOK ☞ *Other devoted lovers include Ferdinand (The Tempest, p. 22), Demetrius (A Midsummer Night's Dream, p. 48), Orlando (As You Like It, p. 62) and Romeo (Romeo and Juliet, p. 96).*

Lorenzo

❝ Sweet soul, let's in, and there expect their coming.
And yet no matter: why should we go in?
How sweet the moonlight sleeps upon this bank!
Here will we sit and let the sounds of music
Creep in our ears: soft stillness and the night
Become the touches of sweet harmony.
Sit, Jessica. Look how the floor of heaven
Is thick inlaid with patines* of bright gold:
There's not the smallest orb which thou behold'st
But in his motion like an angel sings,
Still choiring to the young-eyed cherubins.*
Such harmony is in immortal souls;
But whilst this muddy vesture of decay
Doth grossly close it in, we cannot hear it.*

[*Enter Musicians.*]

Come, ho! and wake Diana* with a hymn!
With sweetest touches pierce your mistress' ear,
And draw her home with music.* **❞**

(*Act 5, scene 1, lines 49–68, with cut*)

GLOSSARY

patines – beautiful surfaces
cherubins – angels
Such harmony… we cannot hear it – there is beautiful music in our souls
but it is hidden inside our human bodies
Diana – the Roman goddess of the moon
draw her home – i.e. make the moon appear (and accompany Portia's
return)

As You Like It

WHO ☞ *Orlando.*

WHERE ☞ *The Forest of Arden.*

WHO ELSE IS THERE ☞ *Adam, his elderly servant.*

WHAT IS HAPPENING ☞ *Orlando has escaped to the Forest of Arden, from his brother who has been plotting against him. His loyal servant Adam, telling him he can go no further and is dying of hunger, lies down exhausted. Orlando tries to cheer him up.*

WHAT TO THINK ABOUT ☞

- *How will the strangeness of the place he is in, and his weariness, affect Orlando's movements?*

- *Where exactly is Adam?*

- *What is Orlando's relationship with his old and trusted servant?*

- *How frightened might he be? Or how courageous?*

- *Why do you think he speaks in prose?*

WHERE ELSE TO LOOK ☞ *Demetrius (A Midsummer Night's Dream, p. 48) and Troilus (Troilus and Cressida, p. 90) are both talking to their elders.*

Orlando

❝ Why, how now, Adam! no greater heart* in thee? Live a little; comfort a little; cheer thyself a little. If this uncouth* forest yield anything savage, I will either be food for it or bring it for food to thee. Thy conceit* is nearer death than thy powers. For my sake be comfortable; hold death awhile at the arm's end. I will here be with thee presently; and if I bring thee not something to eat, I will give thee leave to die: but if thou diest before I come, thou art a mocker of my labour. Well said!* thou look'st cheerly,* and I'll be with thee quickly. Yet thou liest in the bleak air. Come, I will bear thee to some shelter; and thou shalt not die for lack of a dinner if there live anything in this desert.* Cheerly, good Adam! **❞**

(Act 2, scene 6, from line 3)

GLOSSARY

heart – strength, courage
uncouth – wild, unknown
conceit... powers – imagination... strength
Well said! – well done!
cheerly – cheerful
desert – desolate place

As You Like It

WHO ☞ *Orlando.*

WHERE ☞ *The Forest of Arden.*

WHO ELSE IS THERE ☞ *Orlando is alone.*

WHAT IS HAPPENING ☞ *Orlando has escaped to the Forest of Arden, from his brother who has been plotting against him. Before his escape, Orlando has fallen in love with the beautiful Rosalind; so in love that he has been writing poems about her. Here we find him going through the forest and hanging his verses on the trees. He even carves her name in the bark of the trees.*

WHAT TO THINK ABOUT ☞

- *Orlando is young and in love. How does he move through the forest and where does he hang his poems?*

- *Has he already written the poems or does he compose them as he talks?*

- *Have a clear image of Rosalind in your mind. Imagine all the things he loves about her.*

- *Use the last word of the final rhyming couplet, 'she', as a way of giving a strong ending to the speech.*

WHERE ELSE TO LOOK ☞ *Also expressing their love are Romeo (Romeo and Juliet, p. 96), Troilus (Troilus and Cressida, p. 90) and Bassanio (The Merchant of Venice, pp. 54 and 56).*

Orlando

❝ Hang there, my verse, in witness of my love:
And thou, thrice-crownèd queen of night,* survey
With thy chaste eye, from thy pale sphere above,
Thy huntress' name* that my full life doth sway.*
O Rosalind! these trees shall be my books,
And in their barks my thoughts I'll character,*
That every eye which in this forest looks
Shall see thy virtue witness'd everywhere.
Run, run, Orlando; carve on every tree
The fair, the chaste, and unexpressive* she. **❞**

(Act 3, scene 2, lines 1–10)

GLOSSARY

thrice-crownèd queen of night – the moon goddess Cynthia, who is also
    Diana the goddess of hunting, and Hecate the goddess of the night –
    hence her three crowns
huntress' name – Rosalind
my full life doth sway – governs my whole life
character – write
unexpressive – inexpressible

Twelfth Night

WHO ☞ *Antonio, a sea captain.*

WHERE ☞ *The garden of Olivia's house in Illyria.*

WHO ELSE IS THERE ☞ *Duke Orsino, Viola disguised as 'Cesario', and others.*

WHAT IS HAPPENING ☞ *Twins have been shipwrecked and separated on the coast of Illyria. The girl twin, Viola, has disguised herself as a boy, 'Cesario', found employment with the Duke Orsino, and fallen in love with him. Her brother, Sebastian, has got by with the help of Antonio, a sea captain. Through the play the twins have constantly been mistaken for one another resulting in confusion and heartache. Here, at the end of the play, Antonio denounces 'Cesario', believing him to be Sebastian, for not standing up for him when he was arrested.*

WHAT TO THINK ABOUT ☞

- *Position Cesario and Orsino in the space and be clear where they are as you speak.*

- *Antonio genuinely believes Cesario to be his friend Sebastian. He is really angry and upset that his friend will not vouch for him.*

- *Just how much danger has Antonio put himself in to protect Sebastian?*

- *Orsino might have the power of life or death over Antonio. This will affect how Antonio addresses him.*

WHERE ELSE TO LOOK ☞ *Murellus (Julius Caesar, p. 98) also complains against ingratitude.*

Antonio

❝ Orsino, noble sir,
Be pleas'd that I shake off these names you give me.
Antonio never yet was thief or pirate,
Though I confess, on base and ground enough*
Orsino's enemy. A witchcraft drew me hither:
That most ingrateful boy there by your side,
From the rude sea's enrag'd and foamy mouth
Did I redeem.* A wreck past hope he was:
His life I gave him, and did thereto add
My love, without retention* or restraint,
All his in dedication; for his sake
Did I expose myself, pure for his love,
Into the danger of this adverse town;
Drew* to defend him when he was beset;*
Where being apprehended, his false cunning,
Not meaning to partake with me in danger,
Taught him to face me out of his acquaintance,*
And grew a twenty years removèd thing
While one would wink;* denied me mine own purse,
Which I had recommended to his use
Not half an hour before. ❞

(*Act 5, scene 1, lines 75–95*)

GLOSSARY

on base and ground enough – for good and solid reasons
redeem – rescue
retention – reservation
Drew – i.e. unsheathed my sword
beset – set upon
face me out of his acquaintance – deny he knew me
grew a twenty years… would wink – became in an instant as remote as if
    we had not seen each other for twenty years

Twelfth Night

WHO ☞ *Fabian, a servant.*

WHERE ☞ *A space near the house of Countess Olivia.*

WHO ELSE IS THERE ☞ *The rest of the cast – there are over a dozen – but principally Olivia, whose household he serves, and the duped Malvolio, who has just presented the evidence of the forged letter that has humiliated him.*

WHAT IS HAPPENING ☞ *It is the end of the play. After multiple confusions of mistaken identity and practical jokes, the truth is coming to light and all is being resolved: the twins Viola and Sebastian have been reunited, and each has found love (with Orsino and Olivia, respectively). But Fabian has helped Sir Toby Belch and Maria to dupe Malvolio, Olivia's priggish steward, into believing that she is in love with him. At this crisis of confusion and hurt feelings, Fabian here confesses the truth to Olivia.*

WHAT TO THINK ABOUT ☞

- *How does Fabian feel at suddenly becoming the focus of so much attention?*

- *Why is Fabian confessing? Does he feel any guilt at the joke they have played?*

- *What is his status in relation to all the others involved in the prank?*

WHERE ELSE TO LOOK ☞ *Antonio (Twelfth Night, p. 64) also has some explaining to do earlier in the same scene, as does Demetrius (A Midsummer Night's Dream, p. 48) who has to explain events to someone in authority.*

Fabian

❝ Good madam, hear me speak,
And let no quarrel nor no brawl to come
Taint the condition* of this present hour,
Which I have wonder'd at. In hope it shall not,
Most freely I confess, myself and Toby
Set this device against Malvolio here,
Upon some stubborn and uncourteous parts
We had conceiv'd against him: Maria writ
The letter at Sir Toby's great importance;*
In recompense whereof he hath married her.
How with a sportful malice* it was follow'd
May rather pluck on laughter than revenge,*
If that the injuries be justly weigh'd
That have on both sides pass'd. **❞**

(Act 5, scene 1, lines 340–53)

GLOSSARY

Taint the condition – darken the (otherwise joyful) atmosphere
Upon some stubborn and uncourteous parts... conceiv'd against him – on the
grounds of a certain obstinate hostility we encountered in our
dealings with him
great importance – authoritative bidding
sportful malice – playful vindictiveness
May rather pluck on laughter than revenge – should cause laughter rather
than punishment

The Taming of the Shrew

WHO ☞   *Tranio, the servant of Lucentio but here disguised as his master.*

WHERE ☞   *Baptista's house in Padua, in Italy.*

WHO ELSE IS THERE ☞   *The rich citizen Baptista, and others.*

WHAT IS HAPPENING ☞   *Newly arrived in Padua, Tranio's master Lucentio has fallen in love with Baptista's daughter Bianca. Baptista will not let Bianca marry until her older sister Katherine is married – but no one wants to marry Katherine. The only men Baptista will allow in the house are schoolmasters for his daughters. Lucentio has told Tranio to pretend to be him, and go to the house as a suitor to Bianca with a gift of books. Baptista has just asked if he can 'be so bold' as to ask what Tranio / Lucentio is doing there.*

WHAT TO THINK ABOUT ☞

- *No one in Padua knows Tranio or Lucentio, so he does not have to work hard at his disguise.*

- *You might have fun with the lowly servant pretending to be a scholar of Greek and Latin.*

- *You could play the scene without any disguise – as if Tranio were the genuine suitor for Bianca's hand.*

WHERE ELSE TO LOOK ☞   *Launce (The Two Gentlemen of Verona, p. 30) and Launcelot Gobbo (The Merchant of Venice, p. 52) are both servants, but not in disguise.*

Tranio

" Pardon me, sir, the boldness is mine own
That, being a stranger in this city here,
Do make myself a suitor to your daughter,
Unto Bianca, fair and virtuous.
Nor is your firm resolve unknown to me
In the preferment of the eldest sister.
This liberty is all that I request:
That upon knowledge of* my parentage
I may have welcome 'mongst the rest that woo,
And free access and favour as the rest.
And toward the education of your daughters
I here bestow a simple instrument,
And this small packet* of Greek and Latin books.
If you accept them, then their worth is great. **"**

(Act 2, scene 1, lines 81–94)

GLOSSARY

upon knowledge of – once you know
packet – parcel

Pericles

WHO ☞ *Pericles, Prince of Tyre.*

WHERE ☞ *The palace at Antioch.*

WHO ELSE IS THERE ☞ *Antiochus, King of Antioch, the King's daughter, and others.*

WHAT IS HAPPENING ☞ *To win the hand of the daughter of the King of Antioch in marriage, suitors must answer a riddle. Pericles is the latest suitor to come to Antioch in the hope of answering the riddle. All who have come before him have failed the test and been beheaded. In this, the first of two of his speeches in this book, Pericles sees the King's daughter for the first time.*

WHAT TO THINK ABOUT ☞

- *Follow the daughter as she enters and see what has 'inflam'd desire' in Pericles' breast.*

- *What is it that makes Pericles prepared to risk his life for this girl?*

- *Feel the excitement of the moment and find how that affects Pericles' breath, speech, and movement.*

WHERE ELSE TO LOOK ☞ *Bassanio (The Merchant of Venice, pp. 54 and 56) also has a puzzle to solve to win a hand in marriage.*

Pericles

" See where she comes, apparell'd* like the spring,
Graces her subjects,* and her thoughts the king
Of every virtue gives renown to men!
Her face the book of praises, where is read
Nothing but curious* pleasures, as from thence
Sorrow were ever raz'd* and testy* wrath
Could never be her mild companion.
You gods that made me man, and sway* in love,
That have inflam'd desire in my breast
To taste the fruit of yon celestial tree,
Or die in the adventure,* be my helps,
As I am son and servant to your will,
To compass such a boundless happiness! **"**

(Act 1, scene 1, lines 12–24)

GLOSSARY

apparell'd – dressed
Graces her subjects – even the Three Graces (of beauty, grace and
    inspiration) serve under her
curious – exquisite
ever raz'd – forever erased
testy – irritable, short-tempered
sway – govern, 'have sway over'
adventure – attempt

Pericles

WHO ☞ *Pericles, Prince of Tyre.*

WHERE ☞ *The palace at Antioch.*

WHO ELSE IS THERE ☞ *Pericles is alone.*

WHAT IS HAPPENING ☞ *To win the hand of the daughter of the King of Antioch in marriage, suitors must answer a riddle. Pericles is the latest suitor to come to Antioch in the hope of answering the riddle. All who have come before him have failed the test and been beheaded. In this, the second of two of his speeches in this book, Pericles has solved the riddle and realised to his horror that the King is sleeping with his own daughter.*

WHAT TO THINK ABOUT ☞

- *Pericles is left alone and has to decide what to do. Follow his thoughts from disgust at what he has learnt to deciding to escape from Antioch with his life.*

- *What does Pericles now think of King Antioch, the daughter whom he desired, and himself for finding her so attractive?*

- *How quickly does he make his escape?*

WHERE ELSE TO LOOK ☞ *Hamlet (Hamlet, p. 102) is also full of disgust at what he has learnt.*

Pericles

❝ How courtesy would seem to cover sin,
When what is done is like an hypocrite,
The which is good in nothing but in sight!*
If it be true that I interpret false,
Then were it certain you were not so bad
As with foul incest to abuse your soul:
Where now you're both a father and a son
By your uncomely* claspings with your child,
Which pleasures fits a husband, not a father;
And she an eater of her mother's flesh,
By the defiling of her parents' bed;
And both like serpents are, who though they feed
On sweetest flowers, yet they poison breed.
Antioch, farewell! For wisdom sees, those men
Blush not in actions blacker than the night
Will shun no course to keep them from the light.
One sin, I know, another doth provoke;
Murder's as near to lust as flame to smoke.
Poison and treason are the hands of sin,
Ay, and the targets to put off the shame.*
Then, lest my life be cropp'd to keep you clear,*
By flight I'll shun the danger which I fear. **❞**

(*Act 1, scene 1, lines 121–42*)

GLOSSARY

sight – outward appearance
uncomely – improper
the targets to put off the shame – the shields by which criminals deflect
  their guilt
cropp'd to keep you clear – cut down to keep you free of blame

The Histories

Henry IV, Part One

WHO ☞ *Prince Hal.*

WHERE ☞ *His apartment in London.*

WHO ELSE IS THERE ☞ *The Prince is alone.*

WHAT IS HAPPENING ☞ *Henry, Prince of Wales, known as Prince Hal, is son to King Henry IV and heir to the English throne. He appears in Shakespeare's plays Henry IV, Parts One and Two, and again as the King in Henry V. We first see him as a young man whose life is spent drinking and having fun, and watch him grow to become a great king. There are four of his speeches from the three plays in this book and two further speeches in the companion volume, Shakespeare Monologues for Men. In this first speech Hal has just been left alone by his friends. He compares himself to the sun whose brightness is hidden by clouds. One day, he says, he will surprise everyone by abandoning his dissolute behaviour.*

WHAT TO THINK ABOUT ☞

- *Does Hal feel guilty about the way he behaves?*

- *Is he talking just to himself or might he also be addressing the audience?*

- *At the beginning of the speech he is talking at or about his friends who have just left. Find a way to make the transition to his secret plan with your voice and your movements.*

- *Find a way of performing the decisive rhyme of the speech's final couplet.*

WHERE ELSE TO LOOK ☞ *See Hal's other speeches, and how he later behaves as King, in the following pages.*

Prince Hal

" I know you all, and will awhile uphold
The unyok'd* humour of your idleness.
Yet herein will I imitate the sun,
Who doth permit the base contagious clouds
To smother up his beauty from the world,
That, when he please again to be himself,
Being wanted,* he may be more wonder'd at,
By breaking through the foul and ugly mists
Of vapours that did seem to strangle him.
If all the year were playing holidays,
To sport would be as tedious as to work;
But when they seldom come, they wish'd-for come,
And nothing pleaseth but rare accidents.
So, when this loose behaviour I throw off,
And pay the debt I never promisèd,
By how much better than my word I am,
By so much shall I falsify men's hopes;*
And like bright metal on a sullen ground,*
My reformation, glittering o'er my fault,
Shall show more goodly, and attract more eyes,
Than that which hath no foil to set it off.
I'll so offend to make offence a skill,*
Redeeming time* when men think least I will. **"**

(Act 1, scene 2, lines 192–214)

GLOSSARY

unyok'd – unrestrained
wanted – missed, lacked
falsify men's hopes – defy people's expectations
sullen ground – dull background
I'll so offend to make offence a skill – I'll treat my bad behaviour as a
    subtle art
Redeeming time – making up for the time I have wasted

Henry IV, Part One

WHO ☞ *Prince Hal.*

WHERE ☞ *The Battle of Shrewsbury, July 1403.*

WHO ELSE IS THERE ☞ *The dead body of Hotspur, and 'Jack' Falstaff on the ground feigning death.*

WHAT IS HAPPENING ☞ *Henry, Prince of Wales, known as Prince Hal, is son to King Henry IV and heir to the English throne. The Earl of Northumberland has led a rebellion against the King, but has been defeated at the battle of Shrewsbury where Prince Hal kills the Earl's son, Harry Hotspur, in hand to hand combat. Hotspur's last words describe himself as 'food for…', and Hal completes the dead man's sentence.*

WHAT TO THINK ABOUT ☞

- *Place yourself in relation to where Hotspur and Falstaff are lying on the ground.*

- *Hal has just killed a man in a fierce fight. He will be triumphant and exhausted.*

- *There is a big battle raging around him, so Hal will have little time to stop and reflect.*

- *In what ways does Hal's mood change when he notices Falstaff's body? Why does he start rhyming?*

WHERE ELSE TO LOOK ☞ *See Hal's other speeches, and how he later behaves as King below.*

Prince Hal

❝ For worms,* brave Percy. Fare thee well, great heart!
Ill-weav'd ambition, how much art thou shrunk!
When that this body did contain a spirit,
A kingdom for it was too small a bound,
But now two paces of the vilest earth
Is room enough.* This earth that bears thee dead

Bears not alive so stout a gentleman.
If thou wert sensible of courtesy,*
I should not make so dear a show of zeal.
But let my favours hide thy mangled face,
And even in thy behalf I'll thank myself
For doing these fair rites of tenderness.
Adieu, and take thy praise with thee to heaven!
Thy ignominy* sleep with thee in the grave,
But not remember'd in thy epitaph!

[*He sees Falstaff on the ground.*]

What, old acquaintance! Could not all this flesh
Keep in a little life? Poor Jack, farewell!
I could have better spar'd a better man.
O, I should have a heavy miss of thee,*
If I were much in love with vanity!
Death hath not struck so fat a deer today,
Though many dearer, in this bloody fray.
Embowell'd* will I see thee by and by:
Till then in blood by noble Percy lie. **99**

(*Act 5, scene 4, lines 86–109*)

GLOSSARY

for worms – to be eaten by worms in the grave
a kingdom… is room enough – the world wasn't big enough for him when
    he was alive but now two paces' length is enough to bury his body
sensible of courtesy – aware of my praise
Thy ignominy – i.e. the treason of Hotspur's rebellion
have a heavy miss of thee – miss you greatly (appropriately to your
    massive size)
embowell'd – i.e. the removal of a corpse's guts in preparation for its
    embalming

Henry IV, Part Two

WHO ☞ *Prince Hal.*

WHERE ☞ *The Palace of Westminster, 1413.*

WHO ELSE IS THERE ☞ *Hal's father King Henry IV.*

WHAT IS HAPPENING ☞ *Henry, Prince of Wales, known as Prince Hal, is son to King Henry IV and heir to the English throne. Hal is alone with his dying father who is now asleep. Hal sees the King's crown lying next to him on his pillow, reflects on the troubles it causes for whoever wears it, and mistakenly believes that his father has died. He knows that soon he will have to wear it himself.*

WHAT TO THINK ABOUT ☞

- *Does Hal fear becoming king, look forward to it, or what other feelings might he have?*

- *How much of what he says would Hal like his father to hear, and how much would he like to keep private?*

- *Where is the sleeping King, and where the crown? How does Hal pick up the crown and place it on his head?*

WHERE ELSE TO LOOK ☞ *See Hal's other speeches on the previous pages, and how he later behaves as King below.*

Prince Hal

" Why doth the crown lie there upon his pillow,
Being so troublesome a bedfellow?
O polish'd perturbation! Golden care!
That keep'st the ports of slumber open wide
To many a watchful night! Sleep with it now,
Yet not so sound, and half so deeply sweet,
As he whose brow, with homely biggen bound,*
Snores out the watch of night. O majesty!
When thou dost pinch thy bearer, thou dost sit
Like a rich armour worn in heat of day,
That scalds with safety. By his gates of breath*
There lies a downy feather which stirs not:
Did he suspire,* that light and weightless down
Perforce must move. My gracious lord! My father!
This sleep is sound indeed; this is a sleep
That from this golden rigol* hath divorc'd
So many English kings. Thy due from me
Is tears and heavy sorrows of the blood,
Which nature, love, and filial tenderness
Shall, O dear father, pay thee plenteously.
My due from thee is this imperial crown,
Which, as immediate as thy place and blood,
Derives itself to me.* Lo, here it sits,
Which God shall guard; and put the world's whole strength*
Into one giant arm, it shall not force
This lineal honour from me; this from thee
Will I to mine leave, as 'tis left to me. **"**

(*Act 4, scene 5, lines 20–46*)

GLOSSARY

with homely biggen bound – wearing a simple woollen nightcap
gates of breath – i.e. the mouth and nose
suspire – breathe
rigol – ring, circle (of the crown)
Derives itself to me – comes to me by direct inheritance
and put the world's whole strength – i.e. and even if all the strength in the
    world were to be gathered

Henry V

WHO ☞ *King Henry V.*

WHERE ☞ *The English camp in the night before the Battle of Agincourt, October 1415.*

WHO ELSE IS THERE ☞ *The King is alone.*

WHAT IS HAPPENING ☞ *Henry appears as Prince Hal in Shakespeare's plays Henry IV, Parts One and Two, and again as the King in Henry V. We first see him as a young man whose life is spent drinking and having fun, and watch him grow to become a great king. There are four of his speeches from the three plays in this book and two further speeches in the companion volume, Shakespeare Monologues for Men. The previous speeches in this book have followed Prince Hal in the time leading up to his becoming king. In this speech, as King Henry V, he is about to lead the English soldiers into a decisive battle against the French.*

WHAT TO THINK ABOUT ☞

- *Henry is both a king and a warrior. How does this affect his body, posture, and movement?*

- *Though alone, Henry is talking directly to God.*

- *Henry talks of how his father took the crown by force from King Richard II and tells God how he has done his best to make amends. How much does he need God's forgiveness?*

WHERE ELSE TO LOOK ☞ *See Henry's other speeches as Prince Hal on the previous pages.*

King Henry

66 O God of battles! Steel my soldiers' hearts;
Possess them not with fear; take from them now
The sense of reckoning if the opposèd numbers
Pluck their hearts from them.* Not today, O Lord,
O, not today, think not upon the fault
My father made in compassing* the crown!
I Richard's body have interrèd new,
And on it have bestow'd more contrite tears
Than from it issued forcèd drops of blood.
Five hundred poor I have in yearly pay,
Who twice a day their wither'd hands hold up
Toward heaven, to pardon blood; and I have built
Two chantries,* where the sad and solemn priests
Sing still* for Richard's soul. More will I do;
Though all that I can do is nothing worth,
Since that my penitence comes after all,
Imploring pardon. **99**

(Act 4, scene 1, lines 282–98)

GLOSSARY

take from them… hearts from them – remove their capacity for arithmetic
   if the sheer number of the enemy dishearten them
compassing – obtaining
chantries – chapels (where prayers were sung)
still – constantly

Henry V

WHO ☞ *A Boy.*

WHERE ☞ *The battlefield of Agincourt, 1415.*

WHO ELSE IS THERE ☞ *After directing a French soldier to follow his master, Pistol, he is alone.*

WHAT IS HAPPENING ☞ *The Boy has been servant to Pistol, Nym and Bardolph, three comic, cowardly soldiers. Nym and Bardolph have been hanged for stealing. Pistol and the Boy have captured a French soldier. When the Boy translates the soldier's offer of money, Pistol goes off with him, leaving the Boy to reflect on his situation.*

WHAT TO THINK ABOUT ☞

- *How have the Boy's ideas and attitudes been affected by the company he has kept and the war he has taken part in?*

- *How – or why – has he been able to learn French when his elders have not? Does he really think Pistol is a* 'grand capitaine'?

- *He is now alone. What might the future hold for him?*

- *How frightened is he to be at the mercy of the French, with only other boys to guard the camp?*

WHERE ELSE TO LOOK ☞ *Another boy caught up in warfare is the Son (Henry VI, Part Three, p. 86).*

Boy

❝ *Suivez-vous le grand capitaine.** I did never know so full a voice issue from so empty* a heart: but the saying is true, 'The empty vessel makes the greatest sound.' Bardolph and Nym had ten times more valour than this roaring devil i' the old play, that everyone may pare his nails with a wooden dagger,* and they are both hanged; and so would this be, if he durst steal anything adventurously.* I must stay with the lackeys* with the luggage of our camp: the French might have a good prey of us if he knew of it, for there is none to guard it but boys. **❞**

(Act 4, scene 4, lines 44 to end)

GLOSSARY

Suivez-vous le grand capitaine – (French) 'follow the great captain'
empty – i.e of courage or valour
this roaring devil i' the old play, that everyone may pare his nails with a wooden dagger – the Boy is comparing Pistol to the fearsome devil in the old miracle plays, but who presents so little real threat that anyone can clip his claws with a stage-prop dagger.
adventurously – i.e. involving any personal risk
lackeys – hangers-on (or junior servants)

Henry VI, Part Three

WHO ☞   *The Son.*

WHERE ☞   *The battlefield of Towton, March 1461.*

WHO ELSE IS THERE ☞   *The Son is alone with the body of a man he has just killed.*

WHAT IS HAPPENING ☞   *This speech is all we see of this character in the play. We know nothing else about him beyond what is in these words. He enters dragging in the body of a man he has just killed in battle, during the bloody civil conflict known as the Wars of the Roses. On searching the body for money, he realises that it is the body of his own father.*

WHAT TO THINK ABOUT ☞

- *How difficult is it to drag a dead body?*

- *The mood of the speech and the emotions of the speaker change dramatically once the Son realises who he has killed. Give time for the realisation to sink in between 'Who's this?' and 'O God!'*

- *Use the end of a sentence to mark the end of one thought, and allow time for a new thought to come.*

- *When he asks God's pardon, might he adopt the kneeling position of prayer?*

- *The speech ends with the son saying he will not talk any more until he has finished crying. Do not hurry to come out of the scene, even if you have said the final words.*

WHERE ELSE TO LOOK ☞   *Prince Hal (Henry IV, Part One, p. 78) recognises the body of his friend Falstaff.*

The Son

" Ill blows the wind that profits nobody.
This man, whom hand to hand I slew in fight,
May be possessèd with some store of crowns;*
And I, that haply* take them from him now,
May yet ere night yield both my life and them
To some man else, as this dead man doth me.
Who's this? O God! It is my father's face,
Whom in this conflict I unwares have kill'd.
O heavy times, begetting such events!
From London by the King was I press'd forth;*
My father, being the Earl of Warwick's man,
Came on the part* of York, press'd by his master;
And I, who at his hands receiv'd my life,
Have by my hands of life bereavèd him.
Pardon me, God, I knew not what I did!
And pardon, Father, for I knew not thee!
My tears shall wipe away these bloody marks;
And no more words till they have flow'd their fill. **"**

(*Act 2, scene 5, lines 55–72*)

GLOSSARY

crowns – coins
haply – by chance
press'd forth – forced by the pressgang into joining the army
part – side

The Tragedies

Troilus and Cressida

WHO ☞ *Troilus, a Trojan prince.*

WHERE ☞ *Near the palace of King Priam, during the Siege of Troy.*

WHO ELSE IS THERE ☞ *Troilus is alone.*

WHAT IS HAPPENING ☞ *Helen, the most beautiful woman in the world and wife of Menelaus, King of the Greek city of Sparta, has been abducted by Paris and taken to Troy to be his wife. A war has raged for ten years as the Greeks have besieged Troy in an effort to recapture Helen. Prince Troilus is Paris's brother. He is weary of fighting for Helen when all his thoughts are about capturing the heart of the chaste Cressida, and resentful at having to conduct his courtship of Cressida via her uncle Pandarus.*

WHAT TO THINK ABOUT ☞

- *The sounds of war are echoing about him as Troilus tries to think of Cressida.*

- *What does Cressida look like? What images does Troilus have in his mind's eye?*

- *How hopeful is he that Pandarus will be a successful go-between?*

WHERE ELSE TO LOOK ☞ *Other hopeful lovers include Ferdinand (The Tempest, p. 22), Bassanio (The Merchant of Venice, pp. 54 and 56), and Romeo (Romeo and Juliet, p. 96).*

Troilus

66 Peace, you ungracious clamours! Peace, rude sounds!
Fools on both sides! Helen must needs be fair,
When with your blood you daily paint her thus.
I cannot fight upon this argument;
It is too starv'd* a subject for my sword.
But Pandarus – O gods, how do you plague me!
I cannot come to Cressid but by Pandar;
And he's as tetchy to be woo'd to woo
As she is stubborn-chaste against all suit.
Tell me, Apollo, for thy Daphne's love,*
What Cressid is, what Pandar, and what we?
Her bed is India; there she lies, a pearl:
Between our Ilium* and where she resides,
Let it be call'd the wild and wand'ring flood,*
Ourself the merchant, and this sailing Pandar
Our doubtful hope, our convoy and our bark. **99**

(*Act 1, scene 1, lines 91–106*)

GLOSSARY

starv'd – meagre
Apollo… Daphne's love – the Greek god of the sun (and of poetry) who
 vainly pursued the chaste wood-nymph Daphne
Ilium – Troy
flood – ocean
convoy… bark – escort… pilot-ship

Coriolanus

WHO ☞ *A Citizen of Rome.*

WHERE ☞ *A street in pre-republican Ancient Rome.*

WHO ELSE IS THERE ☞ *A company of mutinous citizens armed with staves, clubs and other weapons.*

WHAT IS HAPPENING ☞ *The ordinary people of Rome are starving. They believe that their rulers, the aristocratic 'patricians', are hoarding surplus grain and profiting at their expense. One of their number, the First Citizen, is leading an angry mob and calling on them to take revenge.*

WHAT TO THINK ABOUT ☞

- *Decide on the layout of the scene. Where is the crowd and where is the First Citizen in relation to the others?*

- *How much can the other citizens be relied upon for support? How strongly must he make his case?*

- *What status does the First Citizen hold among the others?*

- *How does his hunger affect his physique and voice?*

WHERE ELSE TO LOOK ☞ *Murellus (Julius Caesar, p. 98) is also addressing a crowd, though one he considers of much lower status. The First Citizen could be thought to be a gender-neutral role (see Introduction, p. 10). Another such Citizen may be found in the companion book of Shakespeare Monologues for Girls.*

First Citizen

❝ Before we proceed any further, hear me speak.
We are accounted poor citizens, the patricians good. What
authority surfeits on would relieve us:* if they would yield us
but the superfluity, while it were wholesome,* we might guess
they relieved us humanely; but they think we are too dear:* the
leanness that afflicts us, the object of our misery, is as an
inventory to particularise their abundance; our sufferance* is a
gain to them. Let us revenge this with our pikes,* ere we
become rakes: for the gods know I speak this in hunger for
bread, not in thirst for revenge. **❞**

(Act 1, scene 1, lines 1–26, with cut)

GLOSSARY

What authority surfeits on would relieve us – the superfluous luxuries of
the ruling class would serve to relieve our own hunger
but the superfluity… wholesome – merely the excess… virtuous and
restorative
dear – expensively maintained
sufferance – suffering, forbearance
pikes – long, bladed poles used as weapons (contrasted with the citizens
being as thin as *rakes*)

Romeo and Juliet

WHO ☞ *Mercutio, kinsman to the Prince of Verona, and friend of Romeo.*

WHERE ☞ *A street in Verona, Italy, at night.*

WHO ELSE IS THERE ☞ *Romeo, his cousin Benvolio, and their friends.*

WHAT IS HAPPENING ☞ *All are on their way to a party, wearing masks and carrying torches. Romeo moans about the pain of being in love. Mercutio tells him that he has fallen under the influence of 'Queen Mab' – the supernatural fairy-spirit of dreams.*

WHAT TO THINK ABOUT ☞

- *Imagine the mood of mystery and excitement as the boys walk through the night on their way to gate-crash a party.*

- *Draw the audience (the others in the scene, but the audition panel audience as well) into the magical world you describe.*

- *Create different atmospheres for different parts of the speech – magical, humorous, warlike – and impersonate the characters of the different dreamers.*

WHERE ELSE TO LOOK ☞ *Other speeches that focus on the supernatural include those of Puck and the Fairy (A Midsummer Night's Dream, pp. 46 and 44 respectively) and Hamlet (p. 102).*

Mercutio

❝ O, then, I see Queen Mab hath been with you.
She is the fairies' midwife, and she comes
In shape no bigger than an agate-stone
On the forefinger of an alderman,*
Drawn with a team of little atomies*
Athwart men's noses as they lie asleep;
Her wagon-spokes made of long spinners' legs,
The cover of the wings of grasshoppers,

The traces of the smallest spider's web,
The collars of the moonshine's watery beams,
Her whip of cricket's bone, the lash* of film,
Her wagoner a small grey-coated gnat,
Not half so big as a round little worm
Prick'd from the lazy finger of a maid;*
Her chariot is an empty hazelnut
Made by the joiner squirrel or old grub,*
Time out o' mind* the fairies' coachmakers.
Sometime she gallops o'er a courtier's nose,
And then dreams he of smelling out a suit;*
And sometime comes she with a tithe-pig's tail
Tickling a parson's nose as 'a lies asleep,
Then dreams he of another benefice;*
Sometime she driveth o'er a soldier's neck,
And then dreams he of cutting foreign throats,
Of breaches, ambuscadoes, Spanish blades,*
Of healths five-fathom deep;* and then anon
Drums in his ear, at which he starts and wakes,
And being thus frighted swears a prayer or two
And sleeps again. **99**

(*Act 1, scene 4, lines 53–95, with cut*)

GLOSSARY

agate-stone… alderman – carved signet ring… town official
atomies – tiny creatures
wagon-spokes… cover… traces… collars… whip… lash – i.e. the
    individual components and equipment of the miniature carriage
    Mercutio describes
the lazy finger of a maid – the fingers of maidservants were proverbially
    thought to breed maggots if not perpetually busy
the joiner squirrel or old grub – i.e. the carpentry effected by the
    burrowing squirrel or drilling larva
Time out o' mind – since before we can remember
smelling out a suit – locating a useful means of advancement at court
a tithe-pig's tail… another benefice – i.e. the country priest aspires to
    further remuneration by the presentation of his annual reward
breaches, ambuscadoes, Spanish blades – gaps in defensive fortifications,
    military ambushes, the finest swords
healths five-fathom deep – toasts drunk from seemingly bottomless glasses

Romeo and Juliet

WHO ☞ *Romeo, son of Lord and Lady Montague.*

WHERE ☞ *The garden outside the house of the Capulet family.*

WHO ELSE IS THERE ☞ *Romeo is alone, then sees Juliet.*

WHAT IS HAPPENING ☞ *The Montague and Capulet families have been feuding for so long that no one remembers why. Romeo and his friends have just gate-crashed a party at the Capulets' house, where Romeo has fallen in love with Juliet, the Capulets' daughter. He hears his cousin making fun of him, and then notices Juliet in her bedroom.*

WHAT TO THINK ABOUT ☞

- *What is it about Juliet that Romeo finds so attractive? Picture Juliet as Romeo talks of her.*

- *Where does Romeo see Juliet and does he keep hidden so that she cannot see him?*

- *How loudly can Romeo speak without being heard?*

WHERE ELSE TO LOOK ☞ *Others head over heels in love are Bassanio (The Merchant of Venice, pp. 54 and 56) and Orlando (As You Like It, p. 62).*

Romeo

66 He jests at scars that never felt a wound.
But, soft! What light through yonder window breaks?
It is the east, and Juliet is the sun.
Arise, fair sun, and kill the envious moon,
Who is already sick and pale with grief
That thou her maid art far more fair than she.
Be not her maid, since she is envious;
Her vestal livery* is but sick and green
And none but fools do wear it; cast it off.
It is my lady, O, it is my love!
O, that she knew she were!
She speaks, yet she says nothing: what of that?
Her eye discourses;* I will answer it.
I am too bold, 'tis not to me she speaks:
Two of the fairest stars in all the heaven,
Having some business, do entreat her eyes
To twinkle in their spheres till they return.*
What if her eyes were there, they in her head?
The brightness of her cheek would shame those stars,
As daylight doth a lamp; her eyes in heaven
Would through the airy region stream so bright
That birds would sing and think it were not night.
See, how she leans her cheek upon her hand!
O, that I were a glove upon that hand,
That I might touch that cheek! **99**

(Act 2, scene 2, lines 1–25)

GLOSSARY

vestal livery – virginal garments
discourses – talks
Two of the fairest… till they return – her eyes sparkle in place of two of
   the most beautiful stars in the night sky, and at their request in their
   temporary absence

Julius Caesar

WHO ☞ *Murellus, a tribune of the people.*

WHERE ☞ *A street in Rome, 45 BC.*

WHO ELSE IS THERE ☞ *His fellow tribune Flavius, and a throng of citizens.*

WHAT IS HAPPENING ☞ *Julius Caesar has defeated Pompey in battle. Murellus, a tribune of the people, elected to represent the interests of the ordinary citizen, is remonstrating with a crowd who are on the streets celebrating Caesar's victory. He reminds them that it is not so long ago that they were celebrating the victories of Pompey.*

WHAT TO THINK ABOUT ☞

- *How large is the crowd that Murellus is addressing? How loudly must he speak to gain their attention?*

- *At what point, if any, does the crowd calm down and listen?*

- *How can you use the three repeated lines beginning with 'And…' for dramatic effect?*

- *Is there any danger from the cheering crowd that he is arguing with?*

- *What is it that makes him so angry?*

- *Is he successful in his speech?*

WHERE ELSE TO LOOK ☞ *The First Citizen (Coriolanus, p. 92) is a self-appointed representative of the people.*

Murellus

❝ Wherefore rejoice? What conquest brings he home?
What tributaries follow him to Rome,
To grace in captive bonds his chariot-wheels?
You blocks, you stones, you worse than senseless things!
O you hard hearts, you cruel men of Rome,
Knew you not Pompey?* Many a time and oft
Have you climb'd up to walls and battlements,
To towers and windows, yea, to chimney-tops,
Your infants in your arms, and there have sat
The livelong day, with patient expectation,
To see great Pompey pass the streets of Rome:
And when you saw his chariot but appear,
Have you not made an universal shout,
That Tiber* trembled underneath her banks
To hear the replication of your sounds
Made in her concave shores?
And do you now put on your best attire?
And do you now cull out* a holiday?
And do you now strew flowers in his way,
That comes in triumph over Pompey's blood?
Be gone!
Run to your houses, fall upon your knees,
Pray to the gods to intermit the plague
That needs must light on this ingratitude.* **❞**

(*Act 1, scene 1, lines 32–55*)

GLOSSARY

Knew you not Pompey? – have you forgotten (the previously popular
    general) Pompey?
Tiber – the river of Rome
cull out – decide on, pick out
intermit the plague... on this ingratitude – suspend the punishment their
    ingratitude will necessarily provoke

Hamlet

WHO ☞ *Laertes.*

WHERE ☞ *Elsinore Castle, Denmark.*

WHO ELSE IS THERE ☞ *Ophelia, Laertes's sister.*

WHAT IS HAPPENING ☞ *Laertes has returned to Elsinore for the coronation of the new king, Hamlet's uncle, but is now about to return to France. Before he departs he gives his sister some brotherly advice about her relationship with Prince Hamlet.*

WHAT TO THINK ABOUT ☞

- *Is Laertes an older or a younger brother? What type of sibling relationship does he have with Ophelia?*

- *Does Laertes know Hamlet? Would he be as protective of his sister, whoever she was going out with?*

- *How keen is Laertes to leave Denmark and get back to his life in France? What is that life like?*

WHERE ELSE TO LOOK ☞ *Claudio (Measure for Measure, p. 38) also has a close relationship with his sister.*

Laertes

❝ For Hamlet and the trifling of his favours,
Hold it a fashion and a toy in blood,*
A violet in the youth of primy* nature,
Forward, not permanent, sweet, not lasting,
The perfume and suppliance* of a minute, no more.
Perhaps he loves you now,
And now no soil nor cautel* doth besmirch
The virtue of his will;* but you must fear,
His greatness weigh'd,* his will is not his own;
For he himself is subject to his birth.
He may not, as unvalued* persons do,
Carve for himself,* for on his choice depends

The safety and health of the whole state,
And therefore must his choice be circumscrib'd
Unto the voice and yielding of that body
Whereof he is the head. Then if he says he loves you,
It fits your wisdom so far to believe it
As he in his particular act and place*
May give his saying deed; which is no further
Than the main voice* of Denmark goes withal.
Then weigh what loss your honour may sustain
If with too credent* ear you list his songs,
Or lose your heart, or your chaste treasure open
To his unmaster'd importunity.*
Fear it, Ophelia, fear it, my dear sister,
And keep you in the rear of your affection,
Out of the shot and danger of desire.* **99**

(*Act 1, scene 3, lines 5–35, with cuts*)

GLOSSARY

toy in blood – whimsical affection
primy – budding
suppliance – pastime
cautel – deceit
will – desire
greatness weigh'd – high status considered
unvalued – unimportant
Carve for himself – choose as he might wish
in his particular act and place – given the demands of his rank and power
main voice – general consensus
credent – credulous, gullible
unmaster'd importunity – unrestrained persistence
keep you in the rear… danger of desire – stay behind the front line beyond
the range of his amorous artillery

Hamlet

WHO ☞ *Hamlet, Prince of Denmark.*

WHERE ☞ *Elsinore Castle, Denmark.*

WHO ELSE IS THERE ☞ *Hamlet is alone.*

WHAT IS HAPPENING ☞ *Hamlet's father has died and his brother, Claudius, Hamlet's uncle, has married Hamlet's mother and become king. Hamlet suspects that Claudius has murdered his father for the crown. To test his suspicions, Hamlet has asked a group of travelling players to put on a play that depicts the murder of a king. Claudius's reaction to the play has now confirmed Hamlet in his suspicions. Hamlet takes his leave of the players, and his thoughts turn to death, vengeance, and his mother.*

WHAT TO THINK ABOUT ☞

- *Feel the scary atmosphere that Hamlet conjures with his words.*

- *How might Hamlet take his revenge on the uncle that he believes murdered his father?*

- *What does he feel about his mother who has married his uncle? Does he believe that she might have been party to the murder?*

- *How might you use the final rhyming couplet (pair of rhyming lines) to end the speech and make an exit?*

WHERE ELSE TO LOOK ☞ *Caliban (The Tempest, p. 24) also plots revenge.*

Hamlet

" Leave me, friends.
'Tis now the very witching time of night,
When churchyards yawn and hell itself breathes out
Contagion to this world: now could I drink hot blood,
And do such bitter business as the day
Would quake to look on. Soft! now to my mother.
O heart, lose not thy nature; let not ever
The soul of Nero* enter this firm bosom:
Let me be cruel, not unnatural:
I will speak daggers to her, but use none;
My tongue and soul in this be hypocrites;*
How in my words soever she be shent,*
To give them seals never, my soul, consent!* **"**

(*Act 3, scene 2, lines 395–406*)

Nero – Roman emperor who murdered his mother
my tongue... be hypocrites – i.e. what he says and what he feels do not
    agree
words... shent – verbally abused
To give... consent – never let me act on my words (i.e. use violence on his
    mother)

www.nickhernbooks.co.uk

facebook.com/nickhernbooks

twitter.com/nickhernbooks